COLLECTING DREAMS

To Dave

with best wishes

from

Ann Whitmer

COLLECTING DREAMS

SUE WHITMER

TATE PUBLISHING
AND ENTERPRISES, LLC

Published by Tate Publishing & Enterprises, LLC
127 E. Trade Center Terrace | Mustang, Oklahoma 73064 USA
1.888.361.9473 | www.tatepublishing.com

Tate Publishing is committed to excellence in the publishing industry. The company reflects the philosophy established by the founders, based on Psalm 68:11,
"The Lord gave the word and great was the company of those who published it."

Book design copyright © 2013 by Tate Publishing, LLC. All rights reserved.
Cover design by Samson Lim
Interior design by Jake Muelle
Illustrations by Kirk Whitmer

Published in the United States of America

ISBN: 978-1-62295-480-3
1. Psychology / Psychopathology / Compulsive Behavior
2. Family & Relationships / Family Relationships
13.02.15

DEDICATION

For those I love.

PREFACE

If you are reading this book, you are an answered prayer. I trust that you will find love, laughter, and encouragement within its pages.

ACKNOWLEDGMENTS

First, I must recognize and thank two late maternal grandmothers: Elsie Lee Russell (mine) and Mary Frances McKinney (my husband's). Elsie was the grandmother I knew. (My paternal grandmother, Mary Esther Currie, passed away when I was a toddler, although I know that she loved me too.) Elsie taught me the value of hard work, and I miss her spirit and wisdom. I received the gift of another grandmother, Mary Frances McKinney, when my fiancé (now husband of many years) introduced me to his family. Mary Frances was a pioneer in her own right, working alongside William Allen White at the *Emporia Gazette* in Emporia, Kansas. Her writings laid the foundation for me to follow in her footsteps and publish this book. Both women were gregarious, strong, resourceful, smart, articulate, God-fearing, and wonderful role models. But they were very different people: Elsie was lively and high-strung; Mary Frances possessed tremendous grace and dignity.

I thank my lucky stars for the day I walked into Christ Church Lutheran in San Francisco and met John Frykman, PhD. John is a Lutheran pastor and psychotherapist who founded the Drug Treatment Program of the Haight Ashbury Free Clinic in San Francisco. John was always willing to share thoughts and helpful insights. He and his late wife, Cheryl Arnold, became friends and extended family. I am blessed.

I also must thank Dr. Paul C. Booker for providing information regarding how to attempt the beginnings of change in the behavior of a hoarder.

Thanks also to my friend, Becky Fischer Post, for entertaining me with the story of her hair-dyeing bonding experience with her husband, Art Post. Their account seemed appropriate to borrow for one of the chapters. Those who know me would agree that there is no way I would have had an original thought in my head about beer bongs, or beer bong tubes, or anything having to do with beer bongs, or beer bong tubes.

There have been many encouragers: Jerry and Kathy Lodriguss, Rosemary Cortez, Paloma Zapata, Deb Arnhold, Colleen Kelly Dawson, Judith Hugg-Eckhard, Tom Eckhard, Adam Servetah, who read an early draft of what is now Chapter Three and provided helpful feedback, Natasha Kuzmanovic, who set me on the right path, and Paul Coulombe, who was the first person to tell me that I was a good writer and could make him laugh. I would like to especially thank my Facebook friends, who served as my test market and provided valuable and helpful feedback and encouragement. Above all, I thank my fellow members of the 1972 graduating class of Salina High School South, Salina, KS for their undying enthusiasm.

And now, thanks particularly to my sisters, Denise and Michelle, who read numerous draft manuscripts and championed this book. My son Evan provided thoughtful comments, and my son Kirk has added to this work with his visual gift. I must also thank my mother-in-law, Kathleen Whitmer, and my husband,

Scott, for the encouragement and support. Finally, to my parents, Richard and Kathryn: thank you for allowing this story to be told.

AUTHOR'S NOTE

There is some truth in this book. But out of respect for the "collector," I have changed names, places, and events to the extent that I am comfortable calling this a work of fiction. The one exception is the story about baby Stephen; only the names have been changed. However, I remind the reader that we are relying on the memory of a nine-year-old child; therefore, there is probably some fuzziness or fiction in my recollection.

The hoarder in the book is a real person, living a real life in a small town somewhere in rural America, who was kind enough to grant consent for the publication of this work. This person recognized that this book may serve as an encouragement to others in similar circumstances.

Where it didn't seem necessary, I didn't do much of my own invention. For instance, the grandma character in the book is portrayed fairly accurately as the beloved character in real life. That was pretty much the way she rolled.

I did embellish other events here and there throughout the book to make it a more interesting story, or I used some events fictitiously, or bent the truth. The latter was done to protect the innocent – or the guilty, as the case may be!

As of this writing, the real-life character of the father in the story has had one more birthday since the wedding. Getting the care he deserved has changed his outlook on life.

CHAPTER ONE

SATURDAY

It had become a strange year, and I could say this even though it was only July. That spring, the associate pastor of a neighboring church had left suddenly under suspicious circumstances; embezzlement was suspected. It was upsetting to me and to the members of my own church because we had helped support that ministry and had watched it grow. Then a neighbor's daughter died of a brain tumor within a few months of the diagnosis, and lastly, a close colleague was fired, leaving me to pick up the pieces at work. This was not the type of year one hoped for on New Year's Eve when there was the promise of twelve fresh, unblemished months ahead and the anticipation of great things to accomplish and the expectation of auspicious new beginnings. If I'd had the advantage of retrospectively looking back on the entire twelve months at year's end, I might have concluded that it was a bad year, but at the moment, it was simply strange. So I wasn't surprised when Allison called me.

It was one of those one-sided conversations in which my sister seemed to keep repeating herself, and I couldn't get a word in edgewise. Dad was living in an area no bigger than five square feet, and his breathing had worsened so that he now needed to use an oxygen tank 24-7. Also we needed to move Mom and Dad into a different home because "Kelly, you wouldn't believe the house!" Allison summed the conversation up with "Mom says the elderberries are blooming, and they are glorious!" I was as confused as I was the day I had walked into the boys' bathroom at school. It was too much to take in all at once. Allison was a nurse in a trauma unit and tended to deal with her stress through laughter. So when she called me all hysterical, going on and on about Dad's tiny living area and quoting Mom about the elderberries, I decided, reluctantly, that I needed to go home. Clearly, it was a cry for help.

I had not spent much time there since the summer after my freshman year in college when I returned to find that Mom had no food in the house except for dried biscuits, old home-canned pickles, and tea (choice of hot or iced, but mostly hot). I lost five pounds the first week.

She spent her days outside, gardening, but whatever she was trying to grow, probably pumpkins, wasn't helping to feed us now as they would not ripen until the autumn, and this was late spring. Her pumpkins were known for miles around. They won prizes at county fairs, and she was able to sell some to local grocers. It was a proper way of making use of her gardening skills and earning a little extra income. She looked cute in her little overalls as she pathetically scraped the dry ground, waving at neighbors as they drove down the country road at the side of the house. It was as if by spending time outside, she could totally remove herself from all that was happening inside the house. Even when she came in for breaks, food was not mentioned unless it was lunchtime. If I'd had money, I would have tried to find a way to go into town to buy some food for us. But I had none, so the three of us suffered in silence. Since I was the oldest at age nineteen, I'd always felt responsible for the younger ones. Allison was nearly three years younger than me, and Reese was nearly five years younger. I considered calling Grandma to see if she could bring us some food. But that was asking quite a lot since she lived about two hours away, and besides, it would have just created a row with Mother, who would then have been very angry with us for tattling on her. I didn't want to think about the consequences, so I cast that idea aside.

Evidently, I had been pretty lucky. The year I was away at college and eating nice dormitory food, my two sisters had been imprisoned with a diet of frozen fish sticks heated in the toaster and saddled with an obligatory routine of washing dishes in the bathtub. There was only a spigot, not a proper faucet in the tub, but at least it worked—because the kitchen sink had not been installed until only shortly before my arrival at the end of the school year. The bathtub water still ran only through the spigot (no faucet just yet), but at least it was reliable running water, and the dishes no longer had to be transported down the hall to be washed.

To further enhance the welcoming atmosphere of my post-freshman-year homecoming, I had a choice of sleeping arrangements: on the couch in the living room, to be awakened at 5:30 a.m. when Mom and Dad got up, or in a twin bed with choice of sister sleeping buddy: Allison or Reese. The family had moved into a much smaller, still unfinished house nearly a year before, and after all this time, Mom and Dad were even now using the bedroom that was supposed to be mine. They were sleeping on a junky, old bedframe that Mom had found in one of the pastures where it should have stayed. You could only get away with a bedframe like that in a place like Provence, France. In Nowhere, Kansas, it was just sad. Most of my belongings were still packed and stowed away somewhere, and worst of all, Reese was using my dear little bed, but probably not at her initiation. This was a creative way to get children to develop their own wings and fly: make their homecoming so unbearable that they never want to come back.

I wasn't happy at the thought of returning now, some thirty-odd years later, but I decided to go back to see if I could be of some assistance. Plus, I was just curious. Surely, the house couldn't be as bad as what Allison had described. Also, I thought maybe I could pick up a few of my belongings while I was there. I had been asking Mom to send me the jewelry box of my youth. My grandmother—the one I had known—had given it to me for my birthday one year. It was creamy white, with a pretty ballerina painted on the top and a pink ballerina inside that rose and danced to a little tune when the lid was opened. "Stardust," I think that was the song. I'd cherished it but had not taken it to college, which would have been a smart move, had I only known.

The flight was relatively uneventful into the quiet Kansas City airport. Allison picked me up, looking like a train wreck, completely disheveled with no make-up. This was not at all her usual put-together self. She was dressed in mismatched hospital scrubs, a too-big pink top and too-small turquoise bottoms, that looked very uncomfortable and appeared as if she had slept in them. I'd always been a fan of clothing that fit perfectly. It looked as though she had come straight from work, except that her hair was wet, and had been thrown up in a careless chignon with wisps of long, damp tendrils trailing around the sides. She looked comfortably cool in spite of her untidy appearance. I'd forgotten how hot the Midwest could be in August.

"What happened to you?"

Allison laughed. "Guy came into the ER complaining of stomach pains. Doc decided to cut into his abdomen, nicked the guy's bowel, and it literally exploded. Stuff came flying out all over. Everybody in the OR ducked except the doctor, who got it straight in the face. I got a little bit of it on my top. Stuff looked like bird poop with little seeds in it. Sorry about that, but I had to shower and change quickly or I wouldn't have been on time for your flight."

"It's okay; better you than me!" I said. I had never had any aptitude at all for medicine and looked up to her even though I was the oldest. Allison was a very tall, stately brunette. I had grown up to be the shortest with a tiny build, and had always been the fairest with strawberry blonde hair and gray eyes. Allison looked like Dad; Reese, the youngest of the three, looked like Mom, bigger boned, taller than me and thin; and I didn't resemble either parent. In fact, for a long time, I thought I might have been adopted.

We began our drive to the farm several hours away.

After making light conversation for awhile, we fell into silence. Lost in our own thoughts, we eventually began talking about the reason for my visit, and Allison gave me a more thorough update. "At least Dad is drinking regular coffee."

I thought back to my youth. Dad had always drunk coffee. Even when he was reading a book, he nearly always had a cup of coffee at hand, along with the ever-present cigarette, which eventually led to the disease he was now battling, Chronic Obstructive Pulmonary Disease (COPD). Although he'd chosen carpentry as a vocation because he liked working with his hands, he was an intellectual man who loved European history. For instance, you could ask him anything about the War of the Roses, or any other historical fact, European or American for that matter, and he'd know the answer. He was also a math whiz and could do multiplication in his head up to six figures. He could easily have won the millionaire show on TV.

Mom was also very intelligent and an avid reader, perhaps more so than Dad. The two of them would rise together very early in the morning, put on a pot of coffee and read the newspaper or a book before Dad would leave for work. I think some of their best times consisted of reading together and drinking coffee.

"What's that supposed to mean, 'Dad is drinking regular coffee'? Mom and Dad were always coffee drinkers."

"Regular coffee supports lung function. When I was having lots of asthma attacks, my doctor suggested that I drink regular coffee."

"What about decaf? Is that as beneficial?"

"I'm not sure. I need the caffeine anyway. It helps me stay awake when I have to work twelve-hour shifts at the hospital."

I'd always been a hard-core tea drinker but started to wonder if I ought to consider switching to coffee for the benefit of my lungs. "So how did they take your suggestion about moving out of the house?"

Allison's eyes teared, and she wiped a stray tendril away from her face. "Kelly, it was awful. Dad started crying and asked us not to take them away from their home. They really like it there even though Mom has complained about it for thirty years. But they can't continue on like this. It's not fair to Dad for his health although I know Mom can't help it."

I pondered this as we drew into Lenape County, home to Mom, Dad, and Reese's family. I looked out the window and began noticing as the intersecting roads flew by like a flipbook story that each road had been given a real name, and the names seemed to be arranged in alphabetical order. When the folks had first moved there, the country roads had been referred to in the local vernacular. Sometimes they were named after families, such as the "Thompson Road" because the Thompson family lived on the road, or the "White Spring Road" because it went toward the little town of White Spring. But even with such vague names, the locals knew exactly which road you meant. "What's up with these real names on the roads?"

"They started doing that for 911. Everyone has to have a regular street address. That's why Mom and Dad don't have a rural route address anymore."

"Ah."

There had been lots of rain. The fields were mainly green, and the rolling hills pushed against the blue Kansas sky. Trees lined many of the side roads. These plantings alongside the ditches had been the work of the Civilian Conservation Corps during the Great Depression, creating jobs and building windbreaks in the process. There were little wisps of high clouds, reminding me of the days we would lie down in the soft grasses and look up at the sky, inventing elephants and dragons out of the cloud formations and dreaming of places far across the skies and seas and far, far away from Kansas.

"What's this about the elderberries?"

She smiled at the memory. "Well, it was really weird. Mom called me up out of the blue one day, said that she loved me and that the elderberries were blooming and they were glorious! Then she hung up."

I shook my head and laughed. "That was it? That's weird."

"Well, you know Mother…"

"Elderberries—are they trees or bushes? What do they look like?"

"I don't know, but they are glorious!"

We were definitely "city" kids misplaced in the country. I couldn't distinguish an elderberry bush—or elderberry tree for that matter—from poison sumac. We turned down Reese's road. It was one of the roads with tree plantings, adding to the sheltered feeling as we drove down toward her house, admiring the tall corn in the adjacent field. We pulled into her canopied yard sliced with a handy U-drive that her husband had forged through the old trees. The air was sweet and fresh, and the grand, white house framed the beginnings of a picture-perfect Kansas sunset.

After we got our luggage out of the car and inside the house, Reese offered us beverages, and as we sat around her kitchen table, she gave us the latest news. "They had been sleeping in their chairs."

Allison and I tripped over each other with a torrent of questions. "What? Sleeping in their chairs? In the living room? Why were they doing that? That must be very uncomfortable."

"Dad's chair reclines. Mom's doesn't. They were doing that because there was no room in the bed. Mom had it piled high full of junk."

I took a sip of my tea. "Really? What about the other bedrooms?"

"Those have been long since forgotten. They keep the doors shut because those rooms are completely full of stuff. It's amazing the second floor of the house hasn't fallen down on the first floor. All that weight must be really stressing the house. Plus, they have all those old library books the library was going to destroy. Those are in the attic. They got new mattresses, you know."

"Well, that's a step, I guess. So they got new mattresses, but they weren't sleeping on them. That doesn't make any sense to me," I said.

"None of it makes any sense," Allison added. "Mom can't control herself, but she knows it isn't the way for her and Dad to be living. When they got the new mattresses, she didn't want to throw out the old ones."

"Why not?"

Reese got up and moved over to the kitchen sink. She looked very tired but was beautiful as always with her fine features, light brown hair and hazel eyes. She had one of those modern "Posh Spice" (Victoria Beckham) hair-dos and a wardrobe to match. With the exception of the eyes, she was nearly a carbon copy of Mother. Mom's eyes were blue. "She didn't want to throw them out because according to her, the old ones were in 'perfectly good condition' even though they were about a hundred years old, pee-stained, and who knows what else. She simply wanted to put the new mattresses on top of the old ones on the bed. She didn't want the furniture people to make the delivery and take away the old mattresses because they would see the way she and Dad have been living."

Allison's dark eyes were unusually bright as she exclaimed, "Dad would have needed a pole vault to get into bed!"

I nearly choked on my tea. "So what happened to the old mattresses?"

"Mom made the boys—Lars and Chip—retrieve and deliver the new mattresses from the store. They had to take a truck into town, pick up the new mattresses, and haul them out to Mom and Dad's. I hope the store took the delivery charge off the bill. The boys talked her out of putting the new mattresses on top of the old ones. She agreed to let them take the old ones out of the house, but she still didn't want to throw them out. She made them put the old mattresses in the car," Reese said.

"In the car?" Unbelievable. "Which car is that?"

"In the old, white Lincoln Continental. You know the one. It was the car that they never bothered to have serviced. Mom blew the engine in it one day when it ran out of oil, and Dad bought her a new car instead of seeing what he could get for that one if he'd have sold it. Now they just leave it in the yard out by the entrance from the road. There's enough room in it for the old mattresses."

Allison added, "That way, if a homeless person happens to be coming down the road and needs a place to sleep, they can just use the car!"

Lord. This was going to be interesting. It sounded like something out of the old TV series, *Green Acres.*

"So what's their reaction going to be when we go over there?"

She continued, "Well, the last time Reese and I were there, Mom just closed herself up, like a butterfly that had gone back into its cocoon. She is very much the victim in this whole deal."

"Like a butterfly back in its cocoon?" I couldn't imagine that.

"Yes, it's hard to describe, but she just completely shut herself in. Right, Reese?" Reese nodded. "Her face spells forgiveness, but she sort of bends her head down in shame and keeps her arms totally down by her sides. Her whole demeanor spells victim."

"But she's always played the victim," I protested. "And she must know that they shouldn't be living this way, otherwise, she wouldn't have had a problem letting the furniture people deliver the new mattresses."

Reese rejoined us at the table. "Like you said, it doesn't make sense."

Allison had done some research about obsessive-compulsive disorder and pulled some information out of her handbag that she had found on medicinenet. com: "Obsessive-Compulsive Disorder: A psychiatric disorder characterized by obsessive thoughts and compulsive actions, such as cleaning, checking, counting, or hoarding."

She looked up. "Mom has the hoarding thing— duh—and here's the rest of what it says: 'Obsessive-compulsive disorder (OCD), one of the anxiety disorders, is a potentially disabling condition that can persist throughout a person's life. The individual who suffers from OCD becomes trapped in a pattern of repetitive thoughts and behaviors that are senseless and distressing but extremely difficult to overcome. OCD occurs in a spectrum from mild to severe, but if severe and left untreated, can destroy a person's capacity to function at work, at school, or even in the home.'"

"Mom could benefit from counseling," I offered.

Reese interjected, "Everyone says that, but she has to decide for herself that she needs it. The Library Board is getting tired of the messes she is leaving there because she won't keep the area neat. The front desk is full of her Story Hour toys, and she doesn't keep them looking orderly. I used to worry that she was viewed as a poor reflection on me and my family, but now I don't worry about it. I think that people just feel that we have no control over our parents, and they accept us for who we are."

Allison added, "I heard on the QT that the Library Board wants to help Mom 'retire.' I told Helen on the Board that if that's the case, then they need to have a nice, big retirement party for her and thank her for all of her help over the years. They want to build a new library and move everything over to the new building except her." Well, that would be one way to handle it. Allison recounted a special she had seen on TV in which a lady who was a hoarder had received help from a psychologist who made house calls. The counselor was able to get her to agree to throw out seven items on the first day the episode was filmed. She was able to part with four used Band-Aids and three used cotton balls. She had taped them inside the medicine cabinet. "She also had a real affection for an old, moldy blueberry bagel. According to her, it was a thing of beauty. After I saw that, I was convinced that the disease really existed and realized that Mom probably really does have some sort of mental illness. I think OCD might be what it is."

Reese asked, "Kelly, what did you find out from your counselor? Is there a good way to go about this?"

I reflected on my conversation with my psychologist. I supposed it might have been a good thing that I was in New York on September 11. Otherwise, I probably wouldn't have ever sought counseling. But in so doing, I'd uncovered a lot of things besides September 11 that had been troubling me. It got so that I looked forward to the weekly sessions. His office was comfortable. There was a contemporary sofa, loveseat, and swivel chair grouped around a glass and metal coffee table that faced a fireplace. I always sat on the sofa—I never felt compelled to lie down on it—and he would sit opposite me on the loveseat. He'd redecorated the place during one of the periods when I wasn't seeing him so frequently. I'd been used to seeing a bright orange-red poster declaring "Stockwell-Oklahoma" behind his head during our sessions. In its place was a very traditional painting of an ocean scene. The postmodern coffee table had been exchanged for an antique. When I commented on the redecorating changes, he'd informed me that most adults don't notice unless they are gifted. The familiar box of tissues was still on the coffee table, and I'd used quite a number of them over the course of my sessions. After I got the call from Allison, I'd decided to get some advice about Mother.

"He said that it sounded like the hoarding aspect of OCD to him, and if that's the case, then everything has to be a negotiation. We have to get her permission before throwing anything out. Also, he said that if they were to build an addition to the house, it would tend to become full unless Mom is able to conquer this hoarding behavior. He also said that once we establish that she's not willing to negotiate, if it's affecting their health, then we need to have a 'pitching party.'"

"So tell me about the house," I said. "You keep saying I won't believe it. Remember, I've been there, albeit thirty years ago." In more recent visits to the farm, I had always stayed with Reese, or sometimes Allison, when she was living in the area. Mom was usually at work, and Dad would come over to Reese's or Allison's to see me. He invariably wanted to show me something from one of his war memorabilia collections, but wouldn't let me go to their house. He would bring it along when he came for a visit. Obviously, he didn't want me to see the house.

"Kelly, you would not believe it. Stuff is piled high, floor to ceiling. Dad can't take a bath. You remember he always looked forward to relaxing in a hot tub at the end of a hard day's work. And you know Dad was never a neat freak, to the extent of perfection, I mean, but he had generally kept his things picked up."

"Yeah, that's right!" I said. Dad had taken great pride in our previous homes of ensuring the lawns were generally well manicured, and he had almost never left books and things lying around. He may have had little areas of his war collectibles, but they were always well arranged. His only real clutter had been the ashtray.

"It bothers him a lot that the house looks like it does now. The upstairs bathroom is full of junk. He said he would take a bath if it were clean, instead of having to try to go downstairs to take a shower. Mom can't even get back to the laundry room and has been washing all their clothes out by hand in the sink."

"So now when he says he smells a goat, he really does mean he smells himself?" That had been an old joke of his—something about smelling a goat then taking a bath and noticing that the goat smell had gone away. Dad had always had a weird sense of humor.

We called Mom and Dad to see if it was still okay for us to come over. I wanted to get the lay of the land to see just how much work would have to be done. We were all concerned about Dad's health, and the environment was most likely not helping. We piled into Allison's car and drove the few miles over to the homestead.

When we came up the drive, the white Lincoln was parked off to the right side, near the verge just as Reese had said. I could see the mattresses pressing against the windows, filling up the car. Just beyond the Lincoln on the right side of the drive appeared to be quite a bit of shredded paper, with some coffee grounds strewn around. Reese noticed the puzzled look on my face. "That's Mom's compost heap."

"But it looks like a bunch of junk. There's no rhyme or reason to it. It's not even enclosed," I protested.

She rolled her eyes.

I looked over toward the little two-story house. What a depressing mess. The yard was completely overgrown. There were probably bodies in the yard, the grass was so tall, and the knee-high weeds were probably hiding other secrets. The Wandering Jew was also taking over from the retaining wall on the left side of the house down to the center path to the front door—or was that even a path? It used to be the main entrance. How did they get in and out of the house? Through the back door? No, look, there's a ladder perched on the left side of the front of the house, going up to Reese's old room. That way? Joke. Half of the rungs were missing, and the ones that were still in place were broken or bent. There was no way it could have been used safely. There was a downspout just to the right of the front door, extending halfway into the yard, instead of being at the usual location of one of the corners. That would explain all the overgrown mess. The yard was getting plenty of water.

Allison and Reese led the way down the "path." I followed, wishing I had worn long pants and hoping I would not go to bed with lots of bug bites. Before entering the house, Allison asked me if I had any Zyrtec. "Yes, I do. Is it really that bad?"

"Trust me, Kelly, you ought to pop one just to be on the safe side. It won't take effect right away, but you should get some in your system." Okay. I swallowed a pill without any water, leaving a disgusting taste in my mouth. We knocked then opened the door, and I was immediately hit with the most awful, overpowering, musty smell, making me entirely forget the pill taste in my mouth. It smelled of old people, coffee grounds, bacon grease, and animal fat, pickles, mold (probably), dust, and the cloying scent of decaying flowers and general neglected detritus. My nostrils and lungs were begging me to leave at the first step. I was almost afraid to breathe the air.

Straight ahead, the entry was entirely cluttered. Old, antique crocks were piled high with books: volumes and volumes of books. There was a pile of thirty-year-old *Reader's Digest* magazines to one side, as well as some boots—mine, unmoved from thirty years ago—I thought I recognized by the entry closet. On the left was a pretty little table; or it would have been had it not been so cluttered, dusty, and cobweb-ridden. A paint-by-numbers special from the late sixties was propped against the wall on the left side of the entry. I vaguely remembered Mom working on that one winter, back when I was in high school, when times were better. There were old Mason jars, rocks, and Sunday school teaching supplies on either side of yet another "path."

We shouted our greetings and then started up the stairs to the living room area. Foot placement was critical because stuff was piled on both sides of each step, leaving only a tiny path up the middle of the staircase. No wonder Dad feared going up and down the stairs. If he were to enter the house through the back door, he could do all of his living upstairs, including bathing, because the house was built into the side of a hill and the back entrance gave onto the upper level of the house. I'd have to see about suggesting that.

People usually didn't drive around back or use the back entrance because it was too much trouble and also because the original cellar steps from the original old homestead had never been properly incorporated into our new house. Our new dwelling had been built on the same site after the old farmhouse had been torn down. There was a door at the foot of the original cellar stairs on the backside of our house that opened directly into the basement. But the cellar steps themselves were open to sky and prairie except for an old piece of plywood covering them, which everyone knew to avoid.

As we came up the front-entry stairs, I could see that the intersecting hallway was full of items Mom couldn't bear to part with, accumulated over years and years of inability to purge anything. There were baskets, wooden carvings, dead flowers in pots, a tiny, decorative wicker wheelbarrow, boxes, more boxes, and cloths—maybe tablecloths—or clothes piled on top of some of the boxes. It just looked like a bunch of cluttered stuff. There were many, many pictures of angels, embroidered angels, angel Christmas ornaments, and angel pins lining the hall. Some of the angels were simply pictures that had been cut out of magazines or Sunday school periodicals and attached using straight pins; others were proper-framed prints hung appropriately. Not a square inch was bare; angels dominated all. I turned to the right at the top of the stairs and peered toward the living room. More angels—everywhere. Angel figurines, angel pictures, angel prints, angels here, and angels there. I tried not to look shocked, but it was very difficult. Angels were blessing the mess.

I counted eighteen dried floral arrangements throughout the dining and living area. There was no rationale to their placement, but mostly, they were on top of piles of other stuff. The dead flowers were still in the vases, way beyond decay and, judging by the dust, had probably been there for years, souvenirs marking bygone celebrations. I vowed never to send fresh flowers again. Like my sisters had said, their belongings were piled floor-to-ceiling, hard to imagine and harder still to experience firsthand. Dad's little area was the only clear spot in the entire living space. It had been hard to imagine, but there it was: five square feet of space. That was the extent of his life, dawn to dusk. There was a path from his area to the kitchen toward the back of the house and a little path down the hallway past the stairwell. The place looked as if it had not been dusted in years. Cobwebs hung from the ceilings, clinging primarily at the juncture with the walls, but there were also some wisps hanging down into the middle of the room, threatening to cloud Dad's coffee. There were cobwebs covering the photos on the walls, and most surprisingly, cobwebs on the angels as well. It appeared to be a place where no life existed, save spiders, but this was where my dad was spending his final days, his golden years; he surely deserved better than this. No wonder Allison had been so upset, and Reese had long since given up. I certainly hadn't done much to help.

Mom was standing in the middle of the room looking at me as if she were about to be the victim of a purse snatching and had just identified the would-be perpetrator. I felt very awkward as I came into the room and felt her blue eyes piercing mine. Even though it was uncomfortably warm in the house, she was wearing her usual big, floaty clothing. Sometimes she wore kimonos or caftans or long skirts and long-sleeved frilly blouses. Mom had adopted that garb within the past twenty years when it seemed she'd begun wishing she had been born around the turn of the last century. In fact, as I came into the room, it struck me that she did rather resemble a butterfly robed in the pale, soft fabric of the moth-eaten pink floral kimono with orange birds. I recognized that as a souvenir Dad had told me he'd brought back from R&R in Tokyo when he had been stationed in Korea. When times had been better, Mother used to wear skinny Mary Tyler Moore pants and, on occasion, had looked very fashionable.

She was taking up space in Dad's little area, and Dad was sitting in his chair, facing away from us, looking toward a desk placed right in the middle of the room that housed his oxygen apparatus. That appeared to be the only available space in the room for him and his equipment. Beyond the desk was a wall system, filled with a TV and lots and lots of books and God knows what else. Old Christmas presents? Was that a new VCR on top of the old one? Some of the items appeared to be in their original boxes. As I was walking up toward Dad, I passed a recumbent bicycle doubling as a closet for his summer clothes. His shirts and pants were either hanging on the bicycle handles or seat or draped over boxes between his surrogate closet and the staircase. He tried to get up but started coughing and slapped his oxygen mask on. "Well, Kelly, it must be

thirty years since you've been home. Welcome home!"
Hugs were exchanged all around. They both smelled
like the house. I hoped I hadn't wrinkled my nose. I
mumbled my thanks and continued my survey. Across
the way, situated in front of the main windows of the
room and almost entirely unseen, was the sofa, cluttered
as it was, full of newspapers, Easter basket makings,
old papers and bills, and other items too untidy and
disarrayed to make out. The mess went from the arms
and seat cushions of the couch halfway up the windows
along the wall. Mom invited me to sit down in her
chair, literally the only other place to sit. I sat. Allison,
Reese, and Mom stood; then we took turns sitting.

During one of the periods when Mom and I were
standing, we went into the kitchen. I had to kick some
empty plastic gallon jugs out of the way, presumably
saved for some Story Hour or Sunday school project.
The vinyl flooring had been completely worn through
in places, and I could see floorboards. It had not been
changed in over thirty years. Cobwebs clung to every
corner. Old, antique canning jars were perched on top
of the cabinets, and cobwebs were hanging from those,
too. Behind some of the jars, I could see an evil black
growth coming out of the wall. Mold? I could not see
the kitchen table, really. There were many, many objects
piled up nearly eye-level around where the table would
be. I supposed if someone were to go through all of the
items, they would eventually find a table underneath it.
I noticed two microwaves to the side of the refrigerator,
one on top of the other. The one on top was no longer
serviceable as a microwave and was being used as extra

cabinet space, Mother informed me. I found the source of the bacon grease smell. There were old tin cans full of the stuff sitting on top of the stove. "I mix that in with the cat food," she said. I felt my stomach lurch.

She caught me staring at the stove on which I'd noticed the bacon grease. Several pickle jars devoid of pickles but still holding the juice were adding to the clutter on the work surface. "I thought I would make Daddy some pickled vegetables. You know the kind he likes. You can make it using old pickle juice if you heat it up in the microwave." I hoped she really wasn't going to do that. Poor Dad. She dug through the microwave-cum-cabinet and showed me some pretty little foils that had once covered tea bags. "I thought I could make little books out of these for Sunday school or something. The trouble is, I save all of this stuff, then I don't have the time or inclination to do anything with it, and when I do have the time to sit down and do something with it, I can't find it. That's my problem." Aha! She knows there is a problem. I asked if I could come back and look for my jewelry box. She agreed.

We walked back into the main room. The conversation was mostly about the little kitten that Mom had rescued from the road. It wasn't clear how he came to be there, but he was very tiny and had been mewing ever so loudly outside. She'd finally been able to coax him over to her and had brought him inside to give him some milk. Dad had named him Killer. I didn't really think the name was appropriate; "Boots" would have been better. His tiny black frame was emboldened by white paws and little white eyebrows and whiskers that seemed to take up his entire face. He was so sweet and adorable, never mind that he served as Dad's entertainment and personal friend. I was entirely smitten with this little cat, and I think Lady Killer was probably a more accurate moniker. Dad had a reach extender—a little handlike claw at the end of a pole—to assist him in his pathetic living space. Killer seemed to enjoy trying to catch the claw when Dad would move the pole around on the floor. The little cat allowed me to hold him, and I enjoyed cuddling him in my arms and listening to him purr.

Allison is allergic to cats—and probably the entire house—so we didn't stay long, maybe a half-hour, before agreeing to have Mom and Dad come over to Reese's the next day. It would be Sunday, and Mom would be playing the organ for a local church then doing ministry work in the afternoon, but we could see them both before she left in the morning.

We said our good-byes and walked back down the stairs, through the "path" in the yard, and out onto the driveway in the dusk. The cicadas were just beginning to hum, and a few birds twittered in the orchard. The evening sun was glinting off the white Lincoln, making it even more obtrusive against the blues, browns, and greens of the prairie. And as I stood there in the soft Kansas dirt with my arms around my sisters, I finally began to cry.

CHAPTER TWO

SUNDAY

Mom and Dad arrived early as Allison and I were sitting at Reese's kitchen table, trying to figure out a way to broach the idea of a massive cleanup, starting with all the books. Reese had already left to go play the organ at the early service for her church. Allison, wearing jeans today and never at a loss for words, started the negotiation process after Mom and Dad were settled with coffee and tea. The round table, with everyone in a position of power, bolstered her confidence. She fiddled with a stray tendril of her hair, sipped some coffee for lung support, and looked over at Mother, who was wearing a long blue floral caftan.

"Mom, we'd like to find a good home for your books. They deserve a good home."

Mom put her teacup down. She looked as offended as if Allison had just slapped her across the face. Evidently, this was not the way to go about it. She glared at Allison as if beginning a staring contest. "My books *are* in a good home."

"But you don't have room for all of them. Can't we see about donating some to charity?"

"I am *reading* them. I am reading them *all*. They are *my* books. They are mine, and I'm going to read them...*all*."

Ah—okay. Dad had said nothing, and we were getting nowhere. This negotiation thing was not going to be easy. But before we dropped the conversation, I noticed Mom's metamorphosis. She completely shut down and closed up, arms at her sides and head slightly bowed as if to say, "You've bruised me mercilessly, but go ahead and hit me some more. I hate myself and love being a victim." Allison had described how she had seen Mom looking as if she were a butterfly with its wings down at its sides, like it was back in a cocoon. I had to agree. Mother had retreated into her chrysalis.

We steered the conversation in a different direction and tried to regain her good graces before she left to play the organ for her church. We chatted briefly, then Mom got in her car, and Dad went up to the American Legion in the little English settlement of New Haven. He had been managing the place and wanted to go account for the previous evening's earnings. As soon as Reese came home, the three of us decided to run over to Mom and Dad's house to begin cleaning up the bathroom, totally ignoring the advice of my counselor, and yes, throwing stuff away without completing the negotiations with Mom first. After all, Dad had said that he'd take a bath if the upstairs bathroom were cleaned up. Shouldn't be too difficult, right?

We took a large supply of big trash bags and prepared for action. The thing about the bathroom wasn't just that it was dirty. It was full. Six large area rugs were rolled up and propped in the tub. Now I understood why Dad couldn't take a bath. I hadn't gone in the bathroom the night before. There was some old

red-brick-patterned kitchen vinyl flooring that was
sort of lining the floor except that it hadn't really been
installed. It curved up against the tub on one side and
against the vanity on the other. There were more dried
floral arrangements throughout. I stopped counting
them. The inside of the vanity was disgusting. Pink
panty liner wrappings were strewn about being saved
for God knew what. To the right of the vanity, upon
entering the tiny room, there was a linen closet of sorts,
except that there were no doors on the thing. The messy
contents were entirely open to view. That was going
to be an altogether different matter. I saw a supply of
cotton balls, old towels and washcloths, and a variety of
medications, most of them probably well beyond their
expiration dates.

I thought about maybe getting some baskets from
Target or Walmart, just the size that would fit the little
shelves. Those would look cute, and it would help the
place look less cluttered. But the main thing was to
get it cleaned up, and the first order of business was
to move the rugs out of the bathtub. How would we
do that, and where would they go? Hmmm. Well, they
might fit in the white Lincoln! That way, a homeless
person happening down the road could have mattresses
and rugs as well! We didn't feel we could negotiate the
corner around the kitchen; otherwise, we might have
considered trying to remove the rugs through the back
door, but even so, we'd still have to make our way down
the hallway, and there didn't seem to be a way to do that
without cleaning it up first. We needed to devote our
energy to the bathroom but did decide to clean some of

the hallway a little, just at the top of the stairs to tidy it up a bit so that it wouldn't look so overwhelming as you came up the stairs. Not that there were many visitors.

So we took the window screen off and shoved all six rugs out the window, one at a time. They were heavy, and my arms were starting to hurt on the fourth one. I wiped the sweat off my nose with my elbow and shoved some more. Reese volunteered to go around to the backyard and drag each one around to the front and haul it down to the white Lincoln while Allison and I kept working inside.

I thought I could get one of the nephews to hook the car up to a tractor and tow the thing out into one of the back pastures. Allison and I voiced random thoughts to each other as we busied ourselves cleaning the bathroom. Reese was certainly taking a long time. Where was she? I wondered if she was having trouble getting the rugs in the car. It did look pretty full with those mattresses shoved in there. Or, maybe she'd decided to take a break. Oh, well, back to business. The dust was about thirty years old. Literally, no joke. I had never seen dust on soap, but there it was—thick, covering little duck-shaped guest soaps that Mom had perched on a miniature soap dish shelf near the top of the shower stall tiling. The soaps had been yellow once; around the sides they had turned pinkish-orange and looked positively garish. There was a ton of stuff in the tub besides the rugs, and we found some Clear Orange and started using that to scrub the tub. It had been neglected so long that the bottom of the tub was rusty and brown in sections.

All of a sudden, we heard Reese coming back into the house, crying hard and bleeding. Poor Reese! What happened? We hadn't heard her cries for help. Oh no! The dreaded cellar! Handy in case of tornadoes, treacherous if you are hauling six rugs out the bathroom window. As Reese was dealing with the heavy rugs, she'd momentarily forgotten about the cellar. The plywood had given way, and she fell down the creepy, old steps. No one heard her cries except for the outside cats who were napping out on the back porch adjacent to the old cellar. Of course, none of them could be bothered to do anything except crane their necks over the side of the opening to see what on earth had caused the racket and so rudely awakened them. When Reese had collected herself and gathered the courage to open her eyes, she found that she was staring up into blue Kansas sky and curious cat faces.

While all this excitement was going on, Allison had found a teaspoon stuck down in a bag of cotton balls. Odd. It looked as if it had been used. It was all oily and gross. She took it into the kitchen, and after we decorated the bathroom with a couple of little baskets we found out in the hallway, we decided to call it quits after that. We'd amassed six large trash bags full of God-knows-what detritus. We took the full trash bags with us and raced back over to Reese's in order to hide and then dispose of them before Mom got home and would see what was being tossed. We knew that if she were on to us, she'd want to go through the trash and salvage as much of it as she deemed important enough to save, which of course would have been all of it.

It wasn't long before she pulled into Reese's yard and came into the house. Our adrenaline was still pumping. She didn't say anything about Reese's wounds. It was probably a good thing because I'm not sure we would have come up with a decent explanation. "Uh…let's see. Well, we were cleaning up the bathroom and shoving your rugs out through the bathroom window, and Reese fell down the cellar when she was trying to take the rugs around to the Lincoln to store them there and nobody noticed, except for the cats…"

We'd discussed how we were going to break the news to Mom about the fact that we'd moved her rugs and tossed and pitched stuff that, well, really should be tossed and pitched. And we'd decided that we all needed to be there together, all for one and one for all, like the Three Musketeers. Mom didn't waste any time getting back into her car and starting over to her house going the long way, which would be her normal way: the way that had the better roads. Allison, Reese, and I were engaged in a Keystone Cops sort of comedy, tripping over each other as we hurried to pile ourselves into somebody's car, anybody's car *fast* in order to arrive at Mom and Dad's house before Mother got there. We felt that we should prepare her for what to expect before she entered her own home. We wanted to have the conversation in their yard, on her turf, instead of at Reese's table again. We thought it might go better that way and be less threatening.

We took the shortcut—or it would have been had there not been so much rain. The side road we were driving down was a bit muddy, and as we were driving along, probably three-quarters of a mile from Reese's house, we saw Mom flying across the intersection we were about to approach, her black Lincoln literally lifting off the ground as she took the slight rise in the road without slowing down. The fact that we were seeing her there meant that she had gone two and a half miles in the space that it had taken us to go three-quarters of a mile. As I saw her Lincoln zooming past, I immediately had a flashback to the movie *101 Dalmatians.* Here was Cruella DeVil.

We pulled into the driveway just behind her, and I said that I would distract her so that she wouldn't go in the house before us. I started asking her about her compost heap while Allison and Reese went on inside. Mother told me that it was convenient to have the compost heap in that particular spot. I asked her if she'd mind if I planted some flowers around it, and she reacted favorably to that. I thought perhaps I could disguise the whole compost heap as part of a new-age garden or something.

As we entered the house and came up the stairs, I noticed Mom's lip had started to quiver and she looked every bit the six-year-old who had just been informed that Christmas had been permanently canceled. She had unbelievably honed in that something was missing in that section of the hallway visible from the stairs. "But where's my basket?" she said, positively trembling. Lord, she was asking about a tiny basket that had been in the hallway. She'd noticed it was missing out of all the junk that was lining the hallway walls. "We did a little cleaning, Mom, and put that little basket in the bathroom to cheer it up a little bit."

She was very tight-lipped as she made her way down the hall with us toward the bathroom. Just how much of a disturbance had been made? She was completely and utterly shocked when she noticed the rugs were missing. We assured her they weren't far, just down in the white Lincoln. We'd needed to empty the bathtub so Dad could take a bath. She turned to the plastic bag full of cotton balls and sensed further infringement. She said nothing but turned on her heel and flitted down the hall as fast as her voluminous caftan would allow. We stood around like dullards, listening to her footsteps moving toward the kitchen, too afraid to move. I thought maybe she was going to go get the paddle she'd used on us as kids and come back and whack us with it. I peeked around and noticed the long fabric catching on various objects as she moved down the hall. But I saw that she did a pretty good job maneuvering around everything, almost as if she were a sightless person who has memorized the way to work.

I shot back in the bathroom when I heard her returning, and the three of us cowered in the corner. She was carrying the same greasy spoon that Allison had found. Our expressions uniformly registered incomprehension. "I've retrieved my *spoon*," she announced, holding it up, as if speaking to a blind set of dimwits she hoped would miraculously obtain vision and intelligence. We watched as she shoved it back in with the cotton balls, unnecessarily roughly, I thought. We finally regained our voices. "What do you use that for, Momma?" She looked very much the exasperated teacher whose goal for the semester was that her three remedial students would finally grasp that one plus one equals two. "I *use* it for the *oil* to put in my *ears*, thank you very *much*."

We went through the litany of changes—not many, just a couple of things rearranged and the tossing of some trash, and Allison told her she had thrown out some old plastic flowers that she herself had given Mom at one time. Of course, Mother had already noticed that those little flowers were missing, and her lips were now in a perfectly straight line. Reese told her that she'd cut herself up when she was taking the rugs out to the car and had fallen into the cellar. "Well, I'm sorry to you," Mom said, without sounding sorry at all, and turned to leave us alone in the evil, clean room.

But the whole thing was sorry. We'd gone about it the wrong way: invested three hours to clean up a tiny bathroom, and all we had to show for it was six nicely rearranged rugs, six big bags of trash, three or four bruised egos, and an angry mother.

Later, after we'd skulked down the stairs with our tails between our legs and had made our hasty good-byes, we stood in Reese's yard and filled our lungs with fresh air. It smelled sweet and expectant after the moldy, cloying house. And as I took in the lovely air, I looked around at the beautiful hues of the prairie and the panoramic horizon of Kansas where earth meets sky for as far as the eye can see.

I embraced my little sisters again, and suddenly the weight of it all hit us as if we'd been bombarded by steel beams from heaven. The three of us began weeping like there was no tomorrow. We wept for the sheer injustice of it all—for Mom's sense of violation and for her helplessness, for good intentions gone badly, and for the mountain of items that would eventually have to be sorted through and dealt with. But mostly, we wept for a man who had said "I do" to a teenage girl all those years ago, and who had really meant it, and who now deserved more than to spend his remaining days in that terrible mess. And with our heads bent low like three downtrodden sunflowers, we felt every bit as horrible as the house had looked. How on earth had it ever become so bad?

CHAPTER THREE

AN UNEXPECTED GIFT

Now that I look back, I believe Mother's hoarding behavior actually may have started around the time our little brother, baby Stephen, joined our family. We had looked very forward to his arrival with great anticipation. But, my first encounter with Stephen was disappointing, especially since I had waited so long. Dad had finally brought Mom home from the hospital with Stephen in tow. I first laid eyes on him in our tiny living room as Mother settled herself into our large rocking chair. Although my parents had said that he would be different, I had trouble getting beyond the fact that his head was much too large for his body. If I had been an adult, I might have tried to think of something politically correct to say that I didn't really mean. Something like, "Oh, what a beautiful baby!" Instead, I was engaged in a child's pursuit of the truth and simply wanted my questions answered. "Why is his head so big, Mommy? Why did God give him to us?"

I wasn't expecting this at all. Stephen had something called hydrocephalus. All I knew was that his head was really big and scary-looking. We weren't allowed to hold him. I think Mom was afraid the weight of his head would be too much, and we would drop him. Stephen was unable to move his head on his own. It was like an anchor, immobilizing him from the neck up.

Mom was huge during her pregnancy. Could it be twins? It was often debated in our little community, and I didn't miss much when the conversation turned to concerns about my family. Mom was so big that she could not walk down the short hall of our small, ranch-style home without hanging onto the walls. She was often sick and became angry when we were playing just a little too loudly. We tried to be quiet, but sometimes I think we were a little noisier than we needed to be mainly because we wanted her to be up and in the same room with us. It wasn't fun when she was in bed and we were trying to entertain ourselves in a different part of the house. She was a great storyteller, and I loved it when she felt like reading books to us.

They didn't really know that anything was wrong until shortly before Stephen was to be born. Because of Mother's size, an X-ray of the baby was taken during what became her last prenatal visit, showing at first sight what appeared to be an enlarged head. This was small-town Kansas in 1963, and an X-ray was the best technology available.

It was going to be awhile before we could see the new arrival, or our mother for that matter. Children weren't allowed to visit the hospital if they hadn't yet reached the magic age of fourteen. But Dad had wanted to provide Mom with a reminder of the three little girls who were waiting at home. He lined us up in front of the kitchen table and took a photograph of us with a Polaroid camera he had borrowed from someone. This wasn't a good sign because it meant that Mom was not coming home right away.

I correctly deduced that something had gone wrong: there had been major complications. Without really knowing why, I secretly worried about how I would prepare meals for my two younger sisters, launder my father's work clothes, keep the house as neat as Mom always had, and continue my studies in the third grade. We had a decorative mail container in the kitchen with sections for bills, letters, and miscellaneous stuff. The bills section was getting a little too full, and I started to worry about that as well.

Help arrived in the form of an angel named Marie Gustafson. She saw to our meals and laundry and cleaned our house. The house always sparkled after Marie had been there, and whenever I came home to our neat and clean house, I was as happy as I was the year that Santa Claus had brought me a Tiny Tears doll for Christmas. That was one less thing to worry about. Marie's husband, Roger, daughters, Sandra and Donna, and son, Warren—my best friend and the most gorgeous creature ever to grace the halls of Ferguson Elementary School—entertained us and treated us like family members. Thank you, Marie; thank you, Gustafsons.

So at that first encounter, our parents told us we would not be able to keep Stephen very long. Seeing to his every need became our sole mission. We ran little errands for him, read to him, played with him, sang to him, and loved him more than anything else. Little songs were written in his honor. My favorite was set to the tune of "Old Time Religion," which was never sung sotto voce:

"Gimme that little *baby Stevie*
Gimme that little *baby Stevie*
Gimme that little *baby Stee…vie…*
He's good enough for me!"

The song was immortalized and was sung ad nauseam with tremendous gusto. What a lucky little boy to have three sweet, silly, older sisters!

We each had a special task to do for Stephen. Allison's job was to read a story to Stephen every day. She was in the first grade and had started learning to read. Stephen heard 167 stories that spring. His favorite was Dr. Seuss' *One Fish, Two Fish, Red Fish, Blue Fish*. Reese was a preschooler, and her job was to select his clothing. With great care, she chose just the right outfits for him to wear. I was tall for my age back then and could reach into Stephen's crib. I would wind up his favorite toy: a musical stuffed Dalmatian with ears lined in red satin. In complete fascination, Stephen would watch the dog's head move back and forth in time to the music. It was as if the dog were living out Stephen's dream of being able to turn his head.

We discovered that having Stephen in our lives was a bit like hitting the lottery. Hydrocephalus is relatively rare, Stephen was a colossal gift, and people suddenly took an interest in us. Stephen reminded them of their own imperfections, of the things that make us all human, of the things that identify us as individuals. People would go away, humbled and grateful for their own health and happiness.

I soon began to see that there was more to Stephen than just a baby with an oversized head. His message was successful in spite of and because of the way he was packaged. Stephen was considered mentally retarded because of his illness, yet he was the most intelligent baby born to my parents. Stephen was a living paradox: a genius trapped in a scarecrow's body. Each day was an assignment, and Stephen did not disappoint a single sunset.

I began noticing that we didn't seem to have as much food in the house as we used to. Evidently there had been a tremendous financial sacrifice when Stephen was born. His hydrocephalus was considered a pre-existing condition and as such, the insurance policy would not cover the first three weeks of his hospitalization. There was a way to get around that, though. He could be considered a hospice case, institutionalized, and left to die. There wasn't much hope, and he wasn't expected to live beyond a few months anyway. If Mom and Dad had decided to put him in hospice, his expenses would have been paid entirely in full. But for all of their other faults, our parents always tried to do the right thing. In this case, the right thing to do was to go deeply in debt, bring Stephen home, and love him as long as possible. What price can you put on love?

My parents were approached by the March of Dimes who had heard of our situation. They arranged for and funded a trip to Denver, Colorado, for surgical evaluation. I got to travel to Colorado with Dad to bring back Mom and Stephen when the tests were completed. I remember waking up in the car that morning upon arrival in Denver and asking Dad why we were on this racetrack! I'd never been to a city quite that big before. The highways and byways were overwhelming, and it seemed that all of the other cars were leaving us in their dust.

The return trip was very long, and the summer afternoon sun beat down in the hot car as we drove eastward back to our little town. Stephen was very sick and kept vomiting. I'd left my crayons on the little shelf behind the backseats just under the rear window. They all melted. The entire trip had been a frustration. The evaluation had revealed many inoperable small blockages in Stephen's brain. Further surgery would be futile; nothing could be done. Stephen's health worsened once we returned home, and he didn't smile much anymore.

I woke up one bright August morning and immediately knew that something was wrong. The house was unusually quiet, and there were men's wet footprints on the carpeting. Someone had entered the house after walking in the dew-laden grass. Mother looked beautiful and fashionable but very sad when I found her in the kitchen. I don't remember much about the next few days except that my aunt purchased a little suit for Stephen, and he looked very sweet lying there in his casket at the funeral service. Dad lifted each one of us up so we could say good-bye. Reese tried to feel under Stephen's back to see if he had sprouted his angel's wings yet. Each of us gave him a kiss.

Our parents didn't seem to like our suggestion of keeping him in a little glass case in one of the bedrooms, and instead, after the service, we drove to the all-too-familiar cemetery where the same sad throng from the funeral home had reconvened. A hole had been dug very near our brother Jason's grave, who had died of SIDS several years previously at six weeks of age. Jason had been born when I was just a toddler, and I remembered very little except making lots of trips to the cemetery. After prayers my mother threw a rose down onto Stephen's casket. Men started shoveling the dirt over it. I looked over to the left and was able to pick the Gustafsons out of the crowd. They were crying along with us.

After the grave was all tidily packed with dirt, we got back in the car, and Dad, through tears of his own, started driving down the gravel road with the three of us protesting loudly in the backseat. And as we drove past the old tombstones and ancient pines toward the exit, I came to realize that this had been the worst day of my life. But lucky for me, I am now able to look back on Stephen's passing with peace because when I was old enough to understand it, my mother told me how it had all happened.

She'd awakened to a sense of urgency that Stephen needed her. He had not cried or even stirred. And when she got to his crib, something very startling happened: for the first time in his life, Stephen turned his head. A miracle. He turned his head to the right and smiled at Mother. It was the only smile in two weeks. As he smiled, Stephen lifted a tiny hand for her to hold. Then he turned his head back toward the ceiling of the room. Yes, a second miracle. Stephen then looked up, and still holding Mother's hand, lifted his left arm toward the almighty, and took in a breath of air that he never released. Love and peace filled the room.

Why did God give Stephen to us? My question was never answered. Although advances in medical research provide a theory or two, it remains a mystery. But no matter: all I can conclude is that I was fortunate to be part of it. The bittersweet brevity changed my heart and fills me still. I delighted in every happy sunrise until the warm Kansas night when the angels came.

There was something else. When Stephen died, I discovered that love is boundless. Death cannot undo what love has done. And that loving someone less perfect, yet somehow better than yourself, will bring unimaginable joy into your life. As our song acknowledged, he had, indeed, been good enough for us all.

Now he dances in eternal light and hears the music of angels. There is triumph in even the tiniest of miracles, and there can be wisdom and strength in a baby's smile.

CHAPTER FOUR
TRYING TIMES

School started a week after we buried Stephen. It was probably hardest on Reese, who was starting kindergarten. I know Mom struggled with whether to keep her home for another year, but she thought that perhaps making new school friends would be helpful. She was wrong. The 1963 – 1964 school year was a terrible year for all of us. I hated the fourth grade then, and as I look back over all my years of schooling, it was absolutely the worst. I hate it even now.

The year for me was punctuated by many whispered conversations between my teacher and my mother. I was told that I was perpetually daydreaming. It was odd, then, that I was assigned to the back of the room for the entire year, which provided ample daydreaming opportunity.

It was also a year of strange events. Periodically there would be civil-defense drills in which we would have to exit the classroom "in an orderly fashion," and go squat down in a line in the hallway with our heads down and hands clasped over the backs of our necks and heads. Citizens of all ages were taught this technique during the Cold War in order to protect themselves in the event of a nuclear blast. The importance of the exercise began to weigh on us the afternoon Mrs. Dawson was called unexpectedly out of the classroom and returned, crying, to inform us that President Kennedy had been shot.

Mom started me in 4-H and Girl Scouts, her versions of grief counseling. The activities were probably more stressful than helpful. We were always late to 4-H because the meetings were some place far out in the country, and she never got good directions. I hated it because she kept getting lost, and I was always arriving late, putting me in the spotlight, which I had never liked. As to scouting, I had to wear an outdated Girl Scout uniform, and it was stressful being under the watchful eye and hearing the snotty comments of those who could afford the better, more current uniforms.

Our grandmother came out to our house every day; she was funny and smart and praised my school accomplishments, which Mother never seemed to get around to doing. I no longer had to take a backseat during Grandma's visits; she parceled out enough love for everybody. Our grandmother was an excellent advocate for us and acted as more of an equalizer in our individual situations than we had realized at the time.

Allison seemed buoyant although her main problems were asthma attacks. Reese had a tough time both at school and at home. She was ridiculed and pushed about at school because her little brother had had a big head. Mother was actually present during one of those occasions but somehow felt powerless to do anything about it. Why wasn't she her daughter's best advocate? At home, Reese was yelled at nearly every day because she was a bed-wetter. She wet the bed every night, and further frustrating Mother, she sucked her thumb.

Mom painted some pepper stuff on her thumbs to try to get her to stop. There seemed to be nothing she could do about the bed-wetting, so Mom tried some unorthodox methods of her own invention that didn't work. Sometimes I would just go outside when that happened. It was best to maintain a low profile.

On weekends, Reese kept trying to get Stephen's cloth diapers out of the hall closet because she felt that Mother needed another baby. She was probably right, but Mom didn't tell us she couldn't have any more children. Mother made a valiant effort of explaining to Reese that she was a big girl in kindergarten and didn't need to wear diapers. If we'd had more room, I suppose Mom might have stored them somewhere out of sight. But as it was, they were very neatly placed in the hall closet well within Reese's reach. As to another baby, the three of us cried every night for a new little brother and kept pestering our parents to make it happen. In fact, I would sometimes wait until I heard the evening train rolling down the tracks a few miles from our little house, then call into the darkness that I had a new name picked out for a new little brother (or sister)! Mom and Dad were always very gracious about my suggestions, even though they would never be adopted.

I was aware that the bills section of the bills, letters, and miscellaneous box was getting pretty full. In fact, there were usually so many envelopes stuffed in there that the bills section began to look like a strange paper fan. I was very disappointed to learn from Mother that Grandma had had to help pay Santa Claus. I hadn't realized that Santa expected payment! I was starting to figure it all out anyway, though. Sometimes I would recognize a scrap of fabric from one of my homemade dresses reinterpreted in a doll's blanket that would appear on Christmas morning. Mother was always very resourceful, but I would have liked for the magic to continue. Bills had replaced the Christmas mystery.

Life for me didn't really return to quasi-normal until the Beatles made the American scene in February 1964 several months after Stephen's death. I remember it very clearly because they were on the *Ed Sullivan Show*, and we were watching TV that Sunday evening in our basement. I thought they were very cool, and Mom thought they were silly. It was the start of our turning to music for therapy. I took it a step further and started collecting anything having to do with the Beatles.

We got an old, used piano, and Mom began teaching the three of us how to play. She also began teaching a few other students and gave little recitals in our living room from time to time. She requested that each of us prepare one piece plus one encore. (We gave the encore whether the audience requested it or not.)

Reese became the darling of the musical talent in the family. She could play the piano by ear (so could I, for that matter, but I was always taking the backseat). When the school did a little production on *The Sound of Music*, the teacher had asked Reese to be the accompanist. She accompanied her first grade class when they sang one of the tunes. There were many straining heads in the auditorium that evening when the parents were all trying to see which kid was the pianist. Reese looked very sweet in her little pixie haircut and red velveteen dress. For the first time in my life, I realized I was proud to have Reese for a little sister and began talking her up to my friends. Until that time I had considered her a nuisance who ate my Easter candy and pooped in the bathtub.

Music really helped us, but a different kind of distraction was even better. A new family moved next door, and it was interesting that our new neighbors were moving to Kansas from Germany. The kids were all younger than me. There were two girls, closer in age to Allison and Reese, and a little boy who was just a toddler. He was a sweet little boy who became a surrogate brother for us. Our grandmother even "adopted" all of the kids as her own grandchildren. They would call her Grandma Leah, which always made me a bit jealous.

The dad, Jared, was a military guy, and he was stationed at Fort Riley, a doable commute from our little town. Occasionally he had to do something called "CQ," and we all had to play very quietly before and after "CQ." I finally asked what that meant. It stood for "Charge of Quarters" and meant that he would be awake for a long time. So before and after CQ, we had to be *very* quiet so he could sleep.

They were always on a strict budget. They often had beans for evening meals the last few days of each month until Jared got his check. Their house was very spare, but attractively decorated with colored water set in various clear glass containers at the windows. The light made colorful shadows on the walls. This decorating scheme, along with the complete absence of books, were the main two differences between their house and ours. Both houses had exactly the same floor plan, but the contents were very different. Our new neighbors were always in tough circumstances but did what they could with their minimal resources to make the place comfortable. However, their house seemed to grow more and more spare as ours continued to grow more and more full. Mom and Dad had joined a book-of-the-month club, and it seemed that books soon started to gather in odd locations throughout our house.

With the exception of the growing collection of books and my Beatles collection, the little ranch house pre-and post-Stephen was nearly always very neat. We didn't have much (except bills), so there was hardly any visible clutter (except the bills, letters, and miscellaneous box). The flooring was hardwood, and I loved it when Mom decided the floors needed to be polished. After she had put the wax down, she would get an old, worn blanket for us to sit on. She would spin the three of us around our little living room, all of us hanging on for dear life and having a great time of it as she "polished" the floors.

My chore was to do the dishes nearly every night using the recommended Girl Scout method. It was a snap using that method (glasses, then silver, then dishes, then pots and pans; rinse, scrub, rinse, dry), but I did notice that sometimes I had trouble putting the pots and pans away because Mother would never throw out any used tinfoil. She would stack it up inside the cupboards and on occasion, when I was replacing a pot or a pan, I would also have to shove back fifteen or twenty old crumply used pieces of tin foil. In addition to the collection of books now taking over the house, Mother had begun saving trivial things like the tin foil. When butter and margarine manufacturers began selling their products in little plastic tubs, Mother started collecting those as well. She also saved every small glass that had previously housed jelly or snack spreads. I sometimes had trouble finding places for all of these items when I was putting them away.

About this time, Mother also taught me how to clean the bathroom, and it became my main responsibility. This was a task of mine that continued throughout high school. Mother really couldn't stand the smell of cleaning solutions, and I didn't mind the chore. Mom always heaped tons of praise on me every time I cleaned it, and it gave me a sense of accomplishment and pride. I always had to move a number of books and magazines out of the bathroom before I cleaned it, though. That was the only part I disliked about the task.

I began noticing that Mother's personality seemed to be comprised of a series of mixed signals. Some days she was cheery and happy to be with us; other days it seemed she didn't want us within her sight, especially me. Allison was her favorite, and Reese was her "little Mozart." She would forget to send school lunch money for me, or would forget school conferences or would forget I had a dance lesson. She would forget to take me to doctor appointments, and they would have to be rescheduled. Sometimes when I came home from school, she would be stretched out on the couch wearing skinny pants and looking dazed. Sometimes she had a book and sometimes she had a glass of wine, or both. She had started drinking Mogen David wine for her health.

Even before baby Stevie's death, Mother had some very trying days and would not seem to be herself. I had had a dog, Lady, a few years before then—back in the first grade, before Stephen. She was a mutt that looked like a lab-terrier mix. She was a pretty little dog and had smooth, short, dark fur, floppy ears, a long tail, and a white star at her throat. We had all been playing one day after school in the front yard that was directly across from an empty, undeveloped field. A flatbed yellow truck with four wheels on each axle sped down the sloping street. It was making quite a racket, and Lady was running alongside the truck, barking at it. "Lady!" I yelled. As soon as I did, I knew it was the wrong thing to do. In fact, I felt that I knew exactly what was going to happen, but her name flew out of my mouth before I could stop myself. Like a good dog, she started to obey, and when she turned around to look at me, the rear axle went over her body, and the impact threw her to the side of the road. When I got to her, there was some blood but also a lot of fluid coming out of her body. And in an instant, the thing I loved most in the world simply vanished.

I ran to get Mom. When I told her what had happened, something snapped, and suddenly my sweet mommy wasn't standing there anymore. In her place I found a raging, yelling, lunatic thing I didn't recognize. She was incensed that she had to drop everything she was doing and bury the stupid dog. When she had finished her diatribe, she grabbed her favorite gardening tool, a sharpshooter. Reese was a toddler then, and I had to watch her while Mom dug hard at the ground. It was a cold spring, and the ground was still a bit frozen. We wrapped Lady in an old, light-blue blanket and put her in the earth, under the weeping willow tree in the backyard. Mother said not another word but scooped Reese up in one arm and the shovel in the other, turned on her heel, and strode back into the house. I followed her, went into the room I shared with Allison, pulled myself onto the top bunk (which was always mine), and cried myself to sleep. No one came in to see if I wanted dinner or to tell me they were sorry about Lady.

Dad, on the other hand, was an altogether different matter. There were no mixed signals with him. His message was, "Go away and stay out of my sight," without uttering a word. We became afraid of Dad. He didn't seem to be the same daddy who had enjoyed playing with Stephen. He would get up early, leave for work—usually while we were still asleep—come home, eat (no conversation at the table), then go lay down on the couch in the little living room, smoke, and read. He would frown at us whenever we came into the room. We were not allowed to ask him any questions. On Saturdays, he would spend the entire day downtown, having coffee with his buddies. Mom would take us along to do the weekly errands. Saturday night was always spent getting our hair washed and preparing for church the next day. On Sunday the girls would go to church, and Dad would stay home and withdraw further into his solitary shell. Sundays were supposed to be a family day, and what that meant was that we were not allowed to play with neighbors or other friends. We had Sunday dinner together as a family, but Dad rarely spent any time with us, aside from meals. During the summer, we were not allowed to speak at lunchtime because that was when Paul Harvey was on the radio. Dad was an avid fan and became extremely angry when we were talking or laughing during the meal, and he couldn't hear the radio.

It was about that time that the Gustafsons moved away, and my world came to an end. Warren was gone.

But things seemed to change for everybody when Jared got called up for a tour in Vietnam. This was horrifying news and would have been anyway, but it was particularly so because Anna had just had a baby boy a few months before Jared received his new marching orders. In the meantime, our little family was going to be undergoing a change of its own. We were going to be moving to a town about thirty miles away. Dad had been commuting back and forth for several years and had decided it was time to move into a new home.

The evening Jared had to leave, we had invited Anna and the children to come spend a few weeks with us in our new home since it was summer and school was out. So everybody had their bags packed, and I marveled at how small Jared's duffel seemed in relation to the time he would be away—probably for a year. Jared was smartly dressed in his uniform, and Anna looked very pretty in a shift dress. Her dark hair was short and stylish, and she was wearing her best makeup. All of the kids were scrubbed clean.

Jared's journey was to begin at the tiny bus station in our little town. That bus station had the best chocolate chip ice cream. The ice cream counter was a big deep freezer. You could see all of the varieties in their freezer containers through the sliding glass on top. There were six flavors: chocolate chip (my favorite), vanilla, chocolate, strawberry, orange sherbet, and raspberry sherbet. We didn't have any that night, but we weren't really thinking about ice cream anyway. The station had been in that location for a very long time. Grandma owned the building across the street. She rented one side to Virginia, who owned a china shop where all of the girls in the little town registered their wedding china, and the other side she rented to a law firm.

The buildings were all built around the turn of the century, and the bus station was still very old-fashioned-looking inside. There were grand wooden benches and ceiling fans that played lazily in the warm summer breeze. It was a peculiar thing, but there was a jukebox inside, and I remember very clearly that someone had put money in for "Till There Was You," a fitting song from the new Meredith Wilson film *The Music Man.*

And while the song played in the background through the screened door of the bus station, Jared said good-bye to everyone in the dusky summer evening out on the street parking between the bus and our car.

He hugged all of the kids and kissed Anna good-bye. And as they kissed, time stood still. It was the most passionate kiss I have ever seen. Their lips met and stayed that way for a long time in a wordless declaration of love and finality. Anna suddenly burst into a shower of tears, and Jared pulled away briefly, hugged her again and then kissed her quickly for one last time. He passed his duffel over to the bus driver, who had been waiting patiently. Jared then boarded the bus, and sat on the side toward us with his misery wrapped up in his face. He waved sadly, and I waved back.

Anna's outburst lasted well beyond the departure of the bus. Somehow we all managed eventually to get in the two cars, and Anna and the kids followed us over to our new house. We had a new project to rally around. Dad was forced to become more social in the role of a host, and this really seemed to be the turning point for him in the wake of Stephen's passing. He was the only person in the family who had not embraced music for therapy.

CHAPTER FIVE

MONDAY

"Get in," he said, "don't mind the mess. Sorry it looks this way; Mom needed extra room for her stuff so she started putting some of it here in my car. I finally just gave up." I surveyed the area stupidly as I stood outside the car, peering into the window, and tried to figure out if it would be better to get in the car butt first or feet first. I opened the door very cautiously. There was literally no place to sit. Papers, envelopes, and general detritus were strewn about. I decided to try the butt-first approach and parked my rear on the slippery seat, which was about twelve inches higher than it should have been because of all the clutter. I slid down a bunch of envelopes and slick newspaper advertisements and caught myself with my feet. As I did so, I suddenly felt something hard on the floor among the debris. I decided to move some of the stuff out of the way so I could figure out where to put my feet and discovered an oxygen tank. It must have been the one Dad was trying to find so he could go get it refilled. That was a lucky thing, because that's what we had planned to do after going to the bank first.

"Mom is mad."

"How do you know she's mad?"

"I know she's mad because she hasn't said anything."

"Oh." I cast thoughts about in my head for something more useful to say, but nothing came.

Dad continued, "I thought about buying a trailer and putting that in the yard on the north side of the house. We could live in that and it'd be clean."

"But Dad, don't you think that it would eventually become full as well?"

"Probably. It was just a thought. We could stay on our land instead of having to move to town like Allison and Reese had suggested. I told them not to get their panties in an uproar. Mom and I can figure things out for ourselves."

"I don't think a move of any kind will solve the problem," I said.

We should have gone about it differently, but now the damage was already done. It's Monday, the day after the massive bathroom cleaning expedition. Mom has negotiated for some time off, and I'll spend Tuesday with her. Maybe she'll be in a better mood then. Today is Dad's day. We are going to be making a deposit at his bank in a neighboring town. It's the "take" from the weekend business at the American Legion. Dad's responsibility of managing the restaurant and bar has been good; he can get out of the stinky house and do some socializing. I noticed that he exercises his mind on a daily basis too. He gets the newspapers in the morning and works the Jumble and starts the crossword puzzle before leaving the house. He checks e-mail, which he is able to do from his chair with a remote keyboard. Web. tv has been a good thing for Dad. I'm on his e-mail distribution list, and he keeps the funny stuff coming.

I had noticed this morning as Dad did the Jumble and crossword puzzle that his fingertips had become "clubbed." Allison had told me to look at his hands. The clubbing of the fingertips is a sign of oxygen deprivation, a result of end-stage COPD. Dad had had beautiful handwriting in his youth and as a young father, but the last letter I got from him nearly broke my heart. The handwriting was almost completely unrecognizable as his. I was drawn out of my musings when Dad looked over at me from the steering wheel.

"I don't think Mom will ever forgive me for moving us to the farm."

"Why do you say that, Dad? Doesn't she say that she's made peace with the whole thing?"

"She says that, but I think she still hates the house. She spends as little time in it as possible. I don't think she'll ever forgive me for moving her from her 'Camelot.'"

We drove past the foul-smelling feedlot—the smell of money, that is—and made our way over to the bank in the little Swedish settlement of Halmstad, Kansas. It's been Dad's bank ever since he had words with his former banker over some sort of collateral and land matter.

The bank people are nice. "Hello, Mr. Jones! How are you today?" they say. They don't seem surprised to see Dad carrying around his oxygen supply. He tries to joke with them, but he delivers the punch line wrong. They smile anyway. He introduces me as his daughter and begins to take out a press release in which I am quoted. He carries the thing around in his wallet. I think it's lost on most people, but he takes advantage of every captive audience. It's been nice to know that he's proud of me. For a long time when I was growing up, I didn't think he even liked me.

We had lunch in the little village of New Haven, set in a tiny vale near the banks of the Alderson River, the largest town nearest our farm. I could see it shining like a jewel against the prairie. The roofs of the little shops winked in the sunlight. It had become an artists' colony of sorts. There were several little stores devoted to old crafts such as weaving, knitting and crocheting, and glass blowing. There was even a proper artist's studio. He did marvelous paintings, mostly of cattle against pretty prairie scenes. I wondered why the town hadn't brought more attention to itself. But instead of encouraging visitors through advertising, the businesses thrived on word-of-mouth. As we approached the town, Dad decided to stop at the little café out on Highway 9 just north of the little vale, set against the protective ridge the highway ran alongside. The site was well protected from the fierce winds of winter, and there was a proper windbreak across the highway. Someone had done a lot of tree plantings a hundred years before.

When we entered the restaurant, there was complete silence as people stared at me. They were recollecting that I was one of the daughters who lived "away." I noticed Dad wrote a check for $8.59 when he paid for the lunch. I asked my brother-in-law, Allen, about it that evening. He told me that everyone writes checks in the local economy; nobody uses cash. There are no ATM machines in the little town, and the bank in town strictly observes "banker's hours," making it somewhat inconvenient to get cash anyway.

We didn't have any other pressing business while we were out and about, so we decided to go back to the farm after lunch. Dad drove the long way around by the little river. There had been lots of rain, and the banks were high. It was very peaceful driving along without too much breeze. The roads were a little firmer but not muddy. We didn't kick up much dust as we made our way toward the farm. Dad started the conversation about Mom again. I told him she could benefit from counseling.

"But how am I going to get her to go?"

"You can't. She has to decide that for herself. I know myself how hard it can be to pick up the phone when you realize you may need help."

"Well, I know she has her problems. But she's sweet, and she's mine. I knew as soon as I laid eyes on her for the first time that she belonged to me. She was the sweetest little honey bunch of stinkweed I had ever met. She was beautiful, your mother. Still is. And kind. I'd never had anyone be that nice to me before. I was such an uncouth young man, just back from Korea. Your aunt used to complain about me and how my army buddies and I would make her life miserable. Just ask her. Oh, yes, I loved your mother very much and have never stopped loving her."

"Dad, I know she loves you, too, but the house is just not healthy, and I know she can't help it. We have to figure out a way to help her and you."

He didn't reply. That was the end of that, but it was pleasing to have normal conversations with him. As a kid, I never thought that would happen. We fell into our own thoughts as we continued our leisurely drive back toward the homestead. It was a pretty day. The sun was brightly shining, and the fields held a promising corn harvest. When we got to the farm, one of Reese's sons, Lars, came over to help Dad get a fan out of the attic. There was a drop-down stairwell in the hallway, which we'd cleared enough so he could get up there and hoist down the fan. Dad asked me to put it in one of the windows in the living room so it could pull some fresh air into the house. The air was very fragrant, and I stayed at the window for a long time, taking in great gulps of the sweet prairie air.

Dad seemed worn out after our little bit of activity. He reclined his chair back and hooked himself up to his oxygen machine. He fell asleep, and as I watched his breathing, I noticed he seemed to have a little bird chest; the pronounced barrel chest was evidence of end-stage COPD. It was scary the way it seemed his lungs labored as bellows, almost overfilling then entirely deflating, waiting a moment as if to question whether it was possible to repeat, then finally filling again. At one point, it looked like he had stopped breathing altogether, and I was perched on the edge of my seat, ready to call 911. When it looked like he was okay, I got busy.

Killer seemed interested in "helping" me clean the living room. I'd decided I would tackle the cobwebs first and then tidy the sofa. Dad had said he'd like to take a nap on the sofa and would do so if it were cleared of the mess. Killer followed me around and jumped up on the sofa whenever I was in the area. He loved it when I would pick him up and speak to his little face. I took a few breaks here and there, and Killer always joined me in Mom's chair for a little catnap.

It gave me an opportunity to reflect on the period of our lives that Mom would look back on as her Camelot. It was when we lived in the house that we had opened to Anna and her family: the house we had moved to after Stephen had died.

CHAPTER SIX
SUNSHINE AND HAPPINESS

It was a comfortable little home built in the craftsman cottage-style, or sometimes known as a bungalow. This California-style living had been popularized around the turn of the last century. Typical of the bungalow, ours had lots of built-ins, such as a marvelous set of bookcases along one of the living room walls, perfect for our growing collection of books, and a little breakfast nook area in the kitchen. The nook was in a back corner of the house with windows at each edge of the corner. We had given our lovely oval chrome-legged fifties-style Formica-topped kitchen table to Jared and Anna along with numerous other possessions when we'd moved, and we now sat around a sweet, little, round, antique table. I had loved that Formica table; it was basically Stephen's home while he was alive. Mother would always perch him in his baby carrier on top of that table, supported by a pile of pillows due to the weight of his head so the carrier wouldn't tip backward. I was a bit surprised that Mom had parted with that table. But we had moved on to a new life in our new home.

The vantage point in our new kitchen was higher up off the ground than most houses, and it was satisfying to look down in the mornings at the blazing orange trumpet vines clinging along the fence we shared with our neighbors to the west. It was a darling little kitchen—all cozy and homey, complete with a pleasant view.

In addition to the marvelous kitchen, we also had another amazing feature in our new house. Ours was technically an "airplane bungalow" because we had a grand bedroom—a "sleeping porch" atop the garage adjoining the back of the house. The sleeping area was accessed by a hidden stairway that was the culmination of a small central hallway off the dining room, representative of the bungalow design. The bungalow's focus was more on the main living area instead of the more private areas of the house; hence, the hiding of the stairway in a secluded hall. The idea with this type of house was that the front porch, which ran the width of the house, also acted as part of the living area. In some bungalows the living rooms were so tiny, and the house so cozy that a Murphy bed was an essential element. Not so with ours. The living area was spacious, or at least seemed so in comparison with the little ranch house we had used to live in.

In warmer climates, the covered front porch of the typical bungalow also became a sleeping area. My sisters and I often took advantage of the experience of outdoor sleeping during the summers. The south-facing porch was relatively secluded, accessed only from the driveway side of the house and up about five or six steps, or roughly three feet higher than the yard. Additionally, it was encased in a pretty, red, open-brick design of about four feet high that acted as a railing around the perimeter of the structure. This allowed minimal views of the porch from the street and just enough coverage for privacy, especially when it was dark. The high shrubs along the front of the brickwork added to the retreat. And our little town was the safest place in the world to be, unlike other places where you had to lock yourself into your own secure cocoon at night.

I enjoyed sleeping on the front porch except for the mosquitoes, and possibly, having to be the person who slept on the two lawn chairs pushed together. One lucky person got the big comfy-cushioned wicker couch, another relatively lucky person got the chaise lounge, which was good unless you tried to sleep on your side (it didn't recline all the way), and the person who had drawn the shortest straw got the two lawn chairs pushed together. Aside from that, it was very pleasant. The summer breezes fanned the leaves on the grand elm trees in the front yard. Watching the leaves stir was very peaceful. We and many of our neighbors had planted fragrant flowers whose scent arrived in gentle wafts as the cool evening approached, flourishing just as dusk turned to night. The entire length of our new street, Yellow Rose Lane, was treed and defined at the end of each block by a tiny island, which featured an old-fashioned street lamp and lots of pretty blossoms, mostly sweet-scented purple and white petunias, courtesy of the city. The street was brick, and this slowed down traffic. So if anyone did manage to take the curves around the islands quickly, which was near impossible, they were unquestionably slowed by the brick street.

Heading westward on our street through the series of islands and three blocks away was a park. It, too, was designed around a central island—a very large one—that housed a koi pond bisected by a Japanese-style walking bridge, pretty shrubbery, a roofed space for club meetings, and plenty of playground equipment. There were picnic tables and grills for the days America honored itself by taking to the barbecue pit. It wasn't a large park, but it was our park, and the pretty setting made it a very attractive place indeed. This had once been the very wealthy part of town.

I had a crush on the paperboy, who always sped by on his way toward the park. I would seem to wake just prior to the newspaper hitting the floor of the porch. Sometimes the "whack" would awaken me if I had been in a very deep sleep, but I would always manage to poke my head up just enough above the brick railing to see him speed away on his bicycle. I loved it when he came to the house to collect the money every month. There was another newspaper that arrived in the evenings, and I liked that boy, too.

Whenever we slept out on the porch, we tried to be inside the house before the milkman came. There was an insulated container on the porch landing at the top of the steps, underneath where the mailbox had been secured to the front side of the house. The container had been supplied by the local milk company that provided milk from local farms. Two or three times a week the milkman would leave a couple of cartons of milk, and we didn't have to buy it from the store.

I had never seen Mother so happy as when she was unpacking everything and finding ideal places for all of our belongings. There were lots of cubbyholes and a very cool laundry chute, all typical of the bungalow design. We also had a large, full basement. Most homes in Kansas either had basements or cellars, which were used for protection during storms or tornado warnings, but also were handy for storage. The basement in our new house was big enough so that Mom and Dad each had their own workroom along with plenty of storage space throughout. They took full advantage of this arrangement, and initially, each parent kept their own personal workspace very neat and uncluttered.

We'd been looking for a house for some time. Mom had insisted that she didn't want a "cracker box" house like our poor little ranch house. Any type of tract housing would not be acceptable. She wanted a house with character. They'd finally found this one, in an ideal part of town that was affordable. She had absolutely glowed when she'd told our grandmother about it and had drawn a little floor plan of how the house would look inside. I couldn't wait to see our new abode.

We were fairly well settled when Anna and her children came to stay with us. There was plenty of room, and we had the option of sleeping on the floor in the air-conditioned living room if it was very hot outside, or sleeping on the front porch if the weather was milder. We all played well together, and the three of us prayed fervently every night for Jared's safe return. Reese also prayed for the Eskimos so that they wouldn't get cold. But mostly we prayed for Jared and all of the other soldiers in Vietnam so they wouldn't get killed.

After a couple of weeks or so, Anna and family went back home, but we saw them frequently throughout the summer, and our grandma also would see them since she was still living in the same little town. We would ask Anna if she'd had a letter from Jared. It was usually "yes," but if it was "no," she would add that she was certain she would receive two letters from him the following day. We continued to see them throughout that year, usually on weekends once school had started. A number of months later, we received some news that made us just as happy as we'd always felt on Christmas morning: Jared was coming home! I heard Dad telling Mom that Jared had wanted Anna to be sure to strap a mattress across her back. I thought it was a very weird image and a strange request, but evidently it meant something to the adults because they were laughing. I decided it wasn't any of my business, so I didn't ask.

We settled into the new house. Mom and I painted my bedroom, which was one of the small ones on the first floor of the house, tucked away at the base of the central hallway and around the corner from the dining room. She got some glossy pink paint on sale, and we painted the walls pink, and the built-in cupboards above we painted white. It became a very pretty room. I had plenty of room for my various collections: my growing assortment of Beatles items, stuffed animals, Archie and Richie Rich comic books, shoes, shoes, and more shoes, and a rather sizeable collection of leather goods: handbags, wallets, and coin purses. Additionally, I had become a collector of gum wrappers. I would fashion them into long, colorful chains in a chevron pattern.

There was an alcove beneath the built-in cupboards. Sometimes I moved my little bed into the cozy alcove, and sometimes I arranged it parallel to the east-facing windows. I enjoyed the flexibility of determining how much floor space I wanted. This became more important as my collections grew, and I eventually found that keeping the bed within the alcove seemed to be the best arrangement.

Mother continued her conversion into a new person as time moved forward. She joined clubs, had coffee with new friends on a daily basis, spent a lot of time on the phone, and sang to that house. In spite of her sensitivity to odors like cleaning products and such, she stripped off the old woodwork and also took down a faux wall in the living room that a previous owner had installed at one end to cover even more built-in bookcases and windows in their attempt to give the house more of a modern 1960s look. Mother took the house back to its historical bones. An interior architect specializing in bungalow restoration would have been extremely satisfied with her work. A couple of years later, the three of us plus Mom stripped off fourteen layers of old wallpaper in the dining room. When we got it all scraped off and were down to bare sheetrock, each of us wrote our names and date on the wall in pencil. It was 1968.

I didn't really like being sick and having to stay at home because it was hard to get Mom's attention. She literally spent hours chatting on the phone to lots of friends. But when she came in to check to see how you were doing, if you wanted something from the store, she was usually happy to run down to the little neighborhood grocery a few blocks away and get whatever it was that you needed.

Mother always looked smart except when she wore surgical stockings, and she did that because her legs hurt from time to time. But she generally took care of her appearance and blossomed in the new community. She was delighted when the welcome wagon came to call on us and gave us all sorts of freebies to help us get acclimated. She kept some of her old piano students but gained many, many more. She was always busy after school every day with lessons in half-hour increments. She was able to keep the former students by driving back to our previous little town every Friday night. Dad was always away working on some new construction job somewhere, so the three of us were left to our own devices for Friday night dinner.

The first time we were charged with making dinner, the menu consisted of macaroni and cheese and dandelion greens. I'm not sure whose idea the dandelion greens were, but we went out to the front yard and gathered some up, which I cooked for us. I'd taken cooking in 4-H so I knew enough to be dangerous. When it came to the macaroni and cheese,

I hadn't realized you had to drain off the water (the package instructions weren't terribly clear, and lest my younger readers wonder why I didn't just make Easy Mac, this was before microwave ovens and other such conveniences were widely available). So we had macaroni and cheese soup. It was pitiful, but we ate it anyway. I was twelve years old and since then have never developed much excitement about cooking because it didn't seem much fun and usually ended with disastrous results. We were always very glad when Mom got back home on Friday nights, usually about ten o'clock.

But Mom herself usually showed no enthusiasm for cooking, and sometimes when Dad was away, we would just have navy beans or black-eyed peas for dinner. For breakfast, we usually made ourselves cinnamon toast accompanied by a glass of orange juice. The school lunch was often the most nutritious meal of the day. I never understood why people complained about the school cafeteria food. But she was surprising in some new ways. I found that I was able to count on her for little things, like when I needed a maroon skirt for pep club. I was shocked when she actually made the effort to see to it that I got the skirt when I needed it. I think I was so used to being let down that I had lowered my expectations of her. The new house was really something. It could alter a personality.

Dad was home on weekends, and even though he was away a lot, he also seemed to go through a sort of metamorphosis. He began attending church. He was more approachable at home, except when Paul Harvey was on the radio, and then we just had to keep our mouths shut. One time at lunch, Reese and Allison started giggling during Paul Harvey's show. Reese was closer and Dad, in a fit of frustration, popped her with the back of his left hand across the mouth and said, "Eat!" She started choking on a cherry tomato. Allison and I slunk down low in our chairs.

Mother said, "Eat! How do you expect her to eat when she has a whole tomato in her mouth?" He apologized after the show was over, which was also after the fear had left Reese's eyes and she could breathe again. The tomato had popped out of her mouth—whole—after Mom had whacked her on the back. We weren't sure which was more shocking: the fact that Reese had nearly choked to death, or the fact that Mom had just grown a pair right before our very eyes and stood up to Dad.

But generally, Dad would speak to us in the evenings and didn't seem to mind too much if we asked him a question or two as he sat in the living room. It seems strange to say, but we began watching TV together as a family. That hadn't happened too much in our other house, our Stevie house. The TV had been in the basement, and Dad had always isolated himself upstairs in the living room, glued to one of his books. The new house seemed to have a transforming effect on him as well.

CHAPTER SEVEN
TUESDAY

It's the Tuesday after the great cleanup at the farm, and I'm spending the day with Mother. She seems to have forgiven us for the intrusion.

She was dressed in her normal flowing garb including long skirt, long-sleeved frilly blouse, and vest—in the middle of August. On this particular day, she was also wearing a Bubba Gump Shrimp baseball cap I recognized from a trip to California, and an ancient pair of Converse All-Stars shoes, which completed the ensemble. I think she wore the baseball cap because she'd had a bad haircut and didn't like it. She'd always worn her hair short for as long as I could remember. Even so, this was not the way she used to dress. But she started dressing this weird way several years after they'd moved to the farm, so the little house on the farm seemed to have altered her personality as well.

We went to the little town of Stockton in neighboring Pennockquaha County to do some shopping. There was a little drugstore in town that also carried gift items. It always smelled of potpourri. When we finished, we took her purchases back to her shabby

Lincoln, full of all sorts of junk, but she managed to find room for the new stuff by simply piling it on top of the old. She wasn't paying attention as she was pulling out of the parking space, and she nearly backed into someone. I think either I was a distraction or she may not have been feeling well because she wanted to eat lunch right after that, and it was barely 11:00 a.m. But she had always been an early riser and ate breakfast at 5:30 a.m., so I supposed an early lunch wouldn't be all that surprising.

I wasn't hungry but had a soft drink and watched her eat her salad. When we were done, we went back to Reese's house out in the country where I had a quick peanut butter and jelly sandwich because by that time it really was time for lunch. This time it was Mom's turn to watch me eat.

She'd found a Victoria's Secret catalogue in Reese's kitchen and started looking through it as she sat at the table with me while I ate my lunch. She flipped through the catalogue and found several crocheted sweaters she liked and wondered out loud how much yarn she'd need if she were to crochet one herself. I noticed as she browsed the catalogue that she would occasionally stop here and there as if some of the photos required greater scrutiny. She finally looked up. Her blue eyes peered at me over her wire-rimmed glasses and she concluded: "I know what Victoria's Secret *is*."

"You do?"

"Yes, I do," she replied very gravely, as if she were about to reveal a sensitive military secret at tremendous personal risk.

"What's that, Momma?"

Mother paused a bit, as if expecting a drum roll, then whispered, "She uses scant amount of fabric."

I swallowed hard and tried not to laugh.

Right after that we decided to go to a hardware store in town because Mom wanted to buy some wallpaper for the bathroom. So apparently our cleaning effort had inspired a little decorating.

As mother drove, I noticed a series of idiosyncratic behaviors whenever she turned a corner. I'd first noticed it at the little pharmacy, and now the same thing was happening again. She went down a block, and then instead of going on into the next block, she decided to go around the first block...slowly. At each of the four corners she looked right, left, right, and left again...slowly...before proceeding. Lord, this could take forever.

We finally parked right outside her hardware store. We went inside and took our time flipping through the wallpaper selections. At one point, she decided she felt a little achy, and even though it was August and very hot outside, her aches and pains seemed to be bothering her. She whipped some Ben-Gay out of her purse and started rubbing that surreptitiously on her chest by slipping her hand through the buttons of the blouse she was wearing. A customer came into the store and walked past us. As he did so, he rubbernecked sharply with a very puzzled look on his face, trying to figure out what the awful smell was, and what the heck the strange lady was doing. The odor seemed to be borne up to the front desk by the new customer because two people at the cashier's station noticeably raised their noses in response.

After an eternity, Mom chose a very pretty wallpaper pattern and bought seven rolls. The cashier was very helpful—I could tell he was trying hard not to wrinkle his nose—and offered to help us carry her purchase out to the car. We decided to handle it ourselves. Her car was just as messy if not more so than Dad's, and I didn't want the man to see it. I thanked him but mentioned that we were parked just out front, and we'd be able to do it. Yes, it's true that your parents can continue to embarrass you, even as an adult.

After we took the new wallpaper to the farm, it was time to go to the library in little New Haven village so Mom could work her shift. I noticed that all of the books were in order, but her librarian desk looked like a complete dump. What a mortifying mess. I could see why the library board wanted to do something about that. I spent time sifting through some books on inter-library loan and amused myself until it was time to go home. We went back to the farm, and I asked if we could clean up the front yard.

We began by sifting through items that the Wandering Jew had completely overtaken. I found an empty gallon coffee can that was buried beneath a particularly deep section of the ground cover and asked Mom if she needed it. She'd been using it to collect rainwater but agreed to throw it out because she had another one nearby. I also found a toilet tank ball, totally rusty and unusable, as well as an old bicycle wheel, all within the thick overgrowth of the Wandering

Jew. I asked her about everything I uncovered and whether she would like to keep or toss them; the real negotiations had begun. It seemed it was much easier for her to handle parting with things that had been buried and had not been under her control in the house. I wondered if perhaps it was because she hadn't made an emotional attachment to the things we found outside. I moved the rickety ladder from the front of the house and took it around to the back behind the old farm buildings. It was of no use at all and might as well be out of sight.

I decided to continue my walk around the back of the farm buildings to see what else was back there. As I did so, I fervently prayed that I would not see a snake. The old Plymouth Barracuda was back there along with other long-abandoned cars and old farm equipment. It was utterly, shockingly, redneck. Lars came over with a plow and took care of some of the overgrowth in the front yard. Then he and I carried some limestone rock up to the front of the house to help with the drainage. As he was lifting one of the rocks, a little, green garter snake slipped out. It was the snake I had been expecting and thankfully, not a big one.

Later that afternoon, Mom took me down to the orchard. She'd planted many of the trees thirty years before. The trees hadn't produced much fruit that year, but some of them had fared better than others. She found a little apple on one of the trees, picked it, and held it up for me to see as if she were demonstrating a new product on TV. Then that sweet, little woman offered it to me as a token of forgiveness. It was almost too cute to eat—pretty red and tinged with green, a McIntosh apple, I think. But I accepted her gift, wiping it on my shirt, and took a bite, relishing its sweet tartness.

As I savored it, I got to thinking that I hadn't always loved my mother. In fact, there was a period of my life in which I hadn't liked her at all. Not one little bit.

CHAPTER EIGHT
APPLIED KNOWLEDGE

Thad Dooley was a very strange little boy. He would go out into the middle of the street and lay down on the warm bricks. The local traffic got used to this phenomenon and knew to proceed with caution around the prettily flowered island off Octavia Street onto Yellow Rose Lane. Thad seemed to like to do this particularly around lunchtime on sunny summer days. He would lie there and watch the soft movement of the leaves that canopied the street. Just as we had grown fond of our little neighborhood, Thad also seemed to be very happy with the environment. It truly was an engagingly beautiful part of town.

Dad was always careful when he came home for lunch. I think on most days he half-expected Thad to be in the street. But he wouldn't have raced around in any case. He was a diligent driver, and the brick paving was a natural speed bump anyway. It was hard to go fast.

Thad had two older siblings: a brother, Barry, who was a little younger than me and the most annoying thing in the world, and a sister, Krista, who was closer in age to Allison. Generally, we played well together, although Barry would never be my favorite person. Their mom was of Norwegian ancestry, and the Dooley kids taught us how to say "Eenie, Meanie, Meinie, Moe" in Norwegian. I think the mutual name-calling that developed between Barry and me may have actually had its genesis there. The last line in Norwegian (according to the Dooley kids) went something like "anna banna boosalop, doosalop." I changed the last word to "Dooley Slop" when Barry started teasing me. He'd had the brilliant notion of calling me "Smelly," which I didn't think was very nice at all.

One fine summer day, Barry rode past me on his bike as I was walking in the proximity of the little island on the end of the block nearest the intersection of Yellow Rose Lane with Octavia Street. As he did so, he hollered "Smelly" at the top of his lungs. When Barry sped up toward me, I was just going to ignore it, but he went around the island again hollering: "Smelly Kelly!" with even greater volume and urgency. Then he peddled back up to where I was walking on the sidewalk and intentionally tried to run me over. I jumped out of the way as he raced around the island again. I watched the motion of the boy on the speeding bike.

We'd learned about the physics concept of inertia in science class at school.

> Inertia: the tendency of an object in motion to remain in motion, or an object at rest to remain at rest, unless acted upon by a force.
>
> —Sir Isaac Newton

An idea was beginning to form in my head.

Barry came around again. "Smelly Kelly, Smelly Kelly! You stink to high heaven, Smelly Kelly!" I was so infuriated that I grabbed his left arm and was able to use the bike's momentum to throw him off. In fact, inertia had just become my new best friend. Barry fell quite a few feet from the bicycle itself, landed on his butt, and started bawling just like a dang baby. I ran over to where he had landed and punched him hard when he was down.

"Don't you ever call me that name, again!" He wasn't really all that hurt, and I think I might have felt badly if he had been; but as it was, he got up, grabbed his bike, and rode his sorry butt home. I didn't worry about it too much because I figured no boy was going to go tell his mom that he'd just been beaten up by a girl, especially a frumpy thing like me.

His drubbing was probably delivered with no more force than that of a woman powdering her nose. Nonetheless, I amazed myself. My victory was as sweet as if I'd kicked his rear end all the way down Yellow Rose Lane and back. I was never very strong or athletic, and I literally had no upper body strength. The only time I ever got *A*s in gym class was when we were either doing archery or trampoline. I was a particular embarrassment to my team during volleyball in that if I ever managed to serve the ball so that it actually sailed over the net, both my team and the other team would cheer. But lacking athletic prowess and upper body strength, the moniker "Smelly" had carried with it an extra dose of adrenaline and had emboldened me: I never heard that word directed at me again.

I suppose I could also credit Reese for the extra dose of courage. She had developed an unhealthy relationship with food in the wake of Stephen's passing and had become a chubby girl. One day, we had been playing down in the neighborhood park when a boy started bothering us. "Hey, Toothpick! French Fry! Burger Queen!" This last remark was a huge mistake because Reese lumbered over to him and struck him in the back of the knee. The boy, who had been standing on a small mound, lost his balance. Reese seized the opportunity to use gravity to her advantage. She grabbed his arm and flipped him over. He landed flat on his back. Wow. Each of us had developed some backbone from somewhere; it certainly did not come from Mother. But, in spite of our discovery of new-found courage, things were still not ideal.

I think each of us continued to harbor some grief, and it manifested itself in different ways in our daily lives. For instance, I pursued my collections with even more abandon. I began running out of surfaces to keep my stuffed animals on. My bed was now completely covered with them. I had to move little animals out of the way every night. It became annoying. My shoe collection had expanded to the point that my closet was full and I now had a big basket full of shoes over in one corner, along with some of my leather goods. The comic book collection was still relatively under control. Some of the books were out on display in a bookcase; others were in boxes on shelves in the closet. The Beatles memorabilia was safely stored in one of the upper cabinets where it could not be disturbed, with the exception of my records, which were housed on a bedside table shelf under my record player. My gum wrapper collection had been put to strategic use, and I now had several long chains adorning various locations of the pink bedroom. I kept one chain above the door and was able to tell if someone had entered without my permission. I knew how to open the door a certain way so as not to disturb the chain; I was the only one who knew the secret. I had become quite a collector, but my collections had remained relatively orderly with the exception of a few loose gum wrappers here and there.

As to Allison, her sleeping habits changed, and all of a sudden she seemed to develop nightmares. I had traded rooms with her, which required quite a bit of effort to move and rearrange all of my collections, and I now shared the large upstairs sleeping porch with Reese while Allison had taken the downstairs bedroom. I'd always liked the location of that little bedroom, tucked away as it was just off the hallway and past the dining room. I'd felt secure. Plus, I'd kept it clean. Living with Reese made it impossible to keep the large sleeping porch tidy; her things were strewn all over the place, especially her shoes, and she had even taken over my side. Eventually, I gave in and joined the clutter party. That was easy since I had amassed quite a few possessions. But Allison seemed to hear all the house sounds down there, and she also seemed particularly affected by an imaginary friend who was always getting in trouble with burglars and boogey men; this notion was manifested in her dreams.

I worried about Allison's nightmares. They concerned me in that I was being awakened to fear of my own whenever she would start her screeching. One night was particularly bad. I awoke to her screams, and then I heard someone banging around downstairs in the dark. I didn't know if it was a burglar or what, but it seemed pretty close to the base of the stairs leading up to the back sleeping porch. After the banging, Allison started screaming again, this time at a specter, which in reality was Dad who'd gone to check on the screaming. He was standing just outside Allison's bedroom door in the pale moonlight, his two spindly colorless legs seemingly suspended by a pair of very whitey tighties.

This whole nightmare deal with Allison was supremely annoying. Reese was generally easy to get along with at night unless you had to sleep with her, in which case, you would most certainly be awakened to a nice warm feeling of liquid enveloping you which would suddenly turn cold and pungent. With the exception of the new food fixation, Reese's physical and emotional reaction to Stephen's passing had not changed. She was still a bed-wetter, and this continued to frustrate mother, even in the new house. But Reese could be annoying in other ways as well. Her constant repetitious attacks at the piano on weekends would drive us crazy because she would play the same song over and over again. But no one complained, not even Dad. I think everyone realized that music had become her coping mechanism: music and food.

But with Allison, I'm not sure which was more bothersome for the family: the nightmares or Mrs. Robert Richardson. Allison had developed a crush on a boy at school whose name was Robert Richardson. She was convinced she would someday marry him. Her love for this young man was so great that she would sign her name as and insist on being called "Mrs. Robert Richardson." It did not matter what you were talking about, if you addressed her specifically as Allison she would not engage in further dialogue with you unless you changed it to Mrs. Robert Richardson. This could go on for a number of minutes. Grandma thought this was particularly inane and would tell her, "*Stop* that silliness!" but most people humored Allison. Even in our new town, people had known about baby Stephen, and I think as a result, had cut her a break.

Allison also suddenly developed a fixation with cleanliness due to an irrational fear of microorganisms and would not touch any food item with her bare hands. She always used a paper towel or napkin to retrieve toast from the toaster, for instance. This behavior grew to the point that she would not take any item of food from anyone, or touch a book or other item that someone was attempting to hand to her. It developed to the extreme in that when Grandma visited with a birthday gift for Allison, my younger sister would not even open her own gift because she couldn't figure out how to open it with napkins.

It was at this point that Mom and Dad had decided that Allison needed to get counseling. They took her to the same therapist in town that Grandma had used once when she sought treatment for depression. The counselor said that Allison's compulsive behavior seemed not to be a thing related to cleanliness as such, but was more related to a perfectionist attribute which develops in some people who have suffered distress or a trauma of some sort, and consequently develop obsessive-compulsive disorder.

It made me wonder privately if I had developed a similar affliction, although certainly not to the extent Allison had. I tended to be a bit of a perfectionist myself. I always felt I had to be among the best and the brightest. Being smart and striving for perfection and excellence were my coping mechanisms. That's how I fed my self-esteem. It would frustrate me no end if I didn't know an answer or if something was out of order. But I never voiced my concern about myself.

As for Allison, she seemed to keep this cleanliness/ perfectionist quality for the most part under control at school in that if a teacher was handing back work papers that had been graded, Allison would accept that paper. I am not sure how she was able to compartmentalize her life that way, but she got by. Lunch, however, was another matter. Allison always made sure to grab plenty of napkins so that she could eat without touching her food. She always went to a remote corner of the cafeteria and ate by herself.

The counseling had helped but Allison told me later that what had saved her from this affliction was the kindness of others. One day a group of friends saw her walking by and waved her over. She wanted to eat with them, but didn't want them to see how she did it with napkins. The school was serving pizza for lunch. Allison shored herself up, said a prayer, and wiped her hands on several napkins. Then she forced herself to eat the pizza with her hands like everyone else. The transformation was remarkable because from that day forward, Allison was able to touch food and other objects again. We traded rooms again; her nightmares vanished. Eventually Mrs. Robert Richardson left us as well. Things got back to "normal" and life was good once more with the usual little daily challenges.

Allison found she could get into mischief, and it was usually in tandem with Reese. One day, I heard some mid-afternoon screaming coming from up in the attic, which was accessible from the large upstairs sleeping porch. I went on upstairs to see what all of the commotion was. Both girls were declaring "Ee! Ee! Ee!" and jerking their heads slightly with each "Ee!" Strange behavior; were they drunk? They had found some canned pineapple that had been in the fridge a little too long and had become slightly alcoholic. That must have been it because Mom had given up her wine after we moved, and there was never any alcohol in the house anymore.

Why was Mom leaving food in the refrigerator for that long? It was always full of stuff that should be thrown away. Really, there was no excuse for it, except that she continued to gad about with her friends and start some new renovation project for the house whenever she felt like it. Or, sometimes she would just sit and read all day, accompanied only by a cup of coffee and a rather sizeable pile of books. She didn't garden as much now because our new yard was much smaller, but on occasion, she would spend a few hours outside.

She never paid much attention to what was going on in the kitchen and sometimes got so involved in her various activities that she would forget to pick me up from school.

It was about this time that I began noticing that Mom and Dad's room was becoming piled full of stuff, extra blankets and the like. This was a bit surprising because Mom had taken such care–when we had first moved in–to find just the right spot for everything. "A place for everything, and everything in its place!" she had once said to me.

Mother's preoccupation with activities outside of actual housekeeping continued to expand. I had sprained an ankle the following spring and had had to use crutches. Our school was laid out in a spider-like design with legs springing out from a central hub, making it very inconvenient to go from class to class. During that time, I discovered that one of the janitors was a particularly rude man. He had never spoken a word to me before at all, but once I began using crutches, he would intentionally seek me out and call out "Crip! Crip!" whenever he saw me. I wasn't happy about the situation one little bit and was especially tired at the end of each day. My arms would be very sore, and I would just want to go home and rest.

One day, Mother did not appear when she should have, and I waited quite a long time outside. I finally had the idea that perhaps she had called the school, and they had made an announcement on the intercom inside, which I wouldn't be able to hear from outside the school. So I hobbled inside and stayed there but kept my eye out for Mom. There was no place to sit near the doors inside, so I stood there, underarms literally raw from the crutches, for a good forty-five minutes.

Finally, I saw her speed up in front of the school with Reese in the backseat. The journey to the car from the school was a very long one, or it seemed so because the sidewalk angled out at the longest possible point to the corner instead of being in a direct perpendicular line out to the street. It gave me plenty of time to work up as much venom as I could in my expression, and I knew it hit home because Reese looked absolutely astounded when I finally reached the car. Mom looked at me and started all sorts of explanations. I did not say a word, but when she was finished speaking, I threw her my most disgusted look. In utter shock she exclaimed, "Kelly, your little eyes!" and I knew at that moment that her old behavior was back; that I would not really be able to count on her again. I thought she'd moved on from all that undependability that had surfaced when Stephen had died. I thought the move into our new house had cured her of that. After all, she'd even remembered to buy me that pep club skirt when I'd needed it! But the old Mom had returned in full force. I thought very hard, but could not think of any event that would have returned her to her old self except grief re-lived. All I could feel was a disappointing sense of pity. After all, I felt it for myself as well.

I'd noticed a couple of days before this happened that a big bottle of Mogen David wine had appeared in the refrigerator. The old mom was definitely back.

CHAPTER NINE
A VERY SATISFYING VENTURE

Life for me seemed to blossom in the tenth grade. Stephen was now in the relatively distant past, and although we remembered him often, the move to the new house had helped us, and we weren't in a constant state of grief or dealing with constant reminders. We still listened to music a lot, and Mom's repertoire of piano students was ever growing. But there were new activities outside of music and new music activities as well. I was in a different school as I had moved up from junior high to high school. I learned to drive and spent hours after school practicing backing out of and pulling into the driveway. I was either in the Plymouth Barracuda or the VW Beetle. And of course, I became very interested in boys.

A national singing group came to town. They were popular in the late sixties, early seventies at the height of the Vietnam War. Their message was about peace. A little local spin-off formed that was called simply *The Band*.

I'd gotten reacquainted with a girl I'd known only peripherally in junior high. We had different interests, but we ended up in English and gym classes together, and because our last names were alphabetically close, we

were always placed together. The teachers would tick
the students off their lists: "Jameson, Jones, Josephson,
Kraft." This was good for me because Mary Catherine
had become involved in *The Band* even though she
wasn't much of a singer. Her enthusiasm more than
made up for her singing ability.

I went to one of the practices, and a gorgeous boy
with dark hair and blue eyes came over and started
chatting me up. He knew Mary Catherine but
introduced himself to me. I began noticing him at
school, and glory be, he called me up within the week
and asked me out!

My whole world revolved around this guy. We
spent hours on the phone, and it was often difficult
for anyone else to get through to us in the hours
immediately following the dismissal of school. (Note
to my younger readers: this was a few decades before
cell phones were invented and everyone had one.) Our
phone was just inside the kitchen near the swinging
door, and I could go inside the kitchen and shut out
the noise from Mom's piano lessons while I had a nice,
long chat. I happened to be on the phone with him one
day when a boy who lived in the neighborhood came
over and interrupted a piano lesson Mom was giving. I
hadn't noticed the knock on the front door. I was still
on the phone, just inside the kitchen. The young man
came in, told me that he'd had trouble reaching me
on the phone, and asked me to go to a dance. I put
my hand over the phone receiver and explained that I
already had a date. He slunk out of the house.

Mother came unglued. "You were very rude to that boy. He will never come back or call you again!" she predicted.

"But, Mom, what was I supposed to do? I'm dating Robbie. I already had a date."

That spring was the best of my life. We went for walks, movies, snacks at Shelly's, and enjoyed each other's company. I was totally in love. It was nice when he finally got his driver's license, and we didn't have to have his dad chauffeur us around anymore. Robbie drove a little blue Ford, which had a peculiar smell inside, but I didn't mind too much since I was so head-over-heels in love. Robbie went on a three-week vacation with his family when the school year ended, and I thought I would just die. His older brother was being called up to go to Vietnam and was stationed in Fort Benning, Georgia. Robbie's family was going to take a trip to the southeastern United States to see him. They went all over the place. Robbie wrote postcards and brought back some sweet souvenirs from his travels. I threw them all out a few months later.

The Band was still practicing over the summer, and that gave us an excuse to see each other outside of normal dating. One night after rehearsal, he walked me to my car. It was dusky and might have been a romantic moment. Instead, he dropped a bomb. "I don't think we should see each other anymore. Are you still going to come to band practice?" I was in a state of complete shock but managed to gather my wits about me and hold back the tears until I got in the car. About halfway home, I discovered I'd been driving with only the parking lights on.

I spent the rest of the summer in a jealous funk. He'd started dating someone else in *The Band*. It wasn't easy to take. There were other boys who seemed to be interested in me, but I just couldn't get over the breakup. I think the thing that bothered me most was that he'd done it with no explanation.

Summer eventually turned into fall, and school started again. I was in a new high school that had just been built, and that put me far away from Robbie during the day. He lived on the other side of town and attended the old high school. I only had to deal with seeing him at band practices in the evenings, and there was no way I was going to quit.

He was disgusting. He seemed to spend all of his time dreaming up new ways to make me miserable. Finally, as the leaves were beginning to turn color, Mary Catherine and I hatched a plan. We were going to go tee peeing. There were a couple of other candidates whose homes we were interested in marking besides Robbie's. The other two targets were girls from *The Band*. Neither was the girl he had started dating. For whatever reason, I had decided to steer clear of that altogether.

The plan evolved very conveniently in that a mutual friend from our school had invited us to her Halloween party. I'd prepared for this event very well. I saved up some babysitting money and on my way over to the party, I bought twelve rolls of toilet paper, a dozen eggs, and various and assorted cans of frozen juice, mostly Safeway brand frozen concentrated orange and pineapple juice, whatever was cheap. The artillery was safely stored in the VW Beetle, the choice of transportation for the evening.

After the party, around 10:00 p.m., we got in the car and went to the first stop. Our adrenaline was racing as we tossed the toilet paper up into the trees in the side yard of the house. There was a streetlight—brighter than usual, I thought—and we found it difficult to stay in the shadows. There weren't too many trees or other hiding places around. It would have been a more satisfying venture if a dog hadn't started barking. This particular dog had a very loud bark and seemed to be starved for neighborhood news that day. He couldn't pass up the convenient opportunity of notifying every other beast in the neighborhood that he had company. Both of us nearly wet ourselves when someone turned on a porch light. We stupidly started whispering madly to each other, as if that were going to help the dogs shut up. A hasty exit back to the car seemed in order, but we ended up frozen behind a couple of trees when a police cruiser made its way down the street. Lord, someone had called the cops.

I am not sure why I hadn't remembered the inconvenience of the VW losing its muffler a week or two before then. Allison and I had been on our way to a rehearsal, and the muffler simply dropped off in the middle of the street. I made her get out of the car and retrieve the thing. I couldn't very well leave the car and get it myself, could I? Poor Allison; it had been hotter than a baked potato, but she usually did what I told her to, and she didn't fail me this time. But I wasn't thinking about any of that when Mary Catherine and I needed to make our getaway to the next targeted location. After what seemed like several hours, the police cruiser left the neighborhood, and we decided it was okay to try to leave the vicinity. The doggone car back-fired a couple of times when I started the thing, and a couple of big bangs shot out of its backside as I started driving carefully down the street. It sounded exactly like gunshots. What a stupid idea! But we decided we must persevere, so we went to the second stop. No dogs this time, but a car did come down the street after we'd gotten out of the VW with our supplies, and we hid in the bushes.

We did our thing with toilet paper and eggs that time. This visit went better: no dogs and no cops, but the car seemed to get louder and louder every time I started the little engine. It was a four-on-the-floor, and you had to pump the accelerator in order to start the car. Why, oh why, hadn't I taken the Plymouth Barracuda? Well, the VW was pretty much mine, it wasn't bright white like the Barracuda, and frankly, what could be more innocent-looking than a little, mint green VW

Beetle? Finally, after much anxiety, we made our way to the stop we'd been anticipating all evening: Robbie's house, and the pièce de résistance: Robbie's car. I had been saving the frozen juice just for that.

Robbie's car was parked in their backyard very near a back alley, which made access very convenient. The setting was even more perfect in that there were big trees in the backyard, possibly doubling as handy hiding places if need be. It was very dark back there; streetlights were present only on proper streets, not alleys. Conditions were ideal. Why Mary Catherine agreed to this particular piece of the plan definitely spoke to her loyalty to me because she and Robbie were pretty good friends. They had a number of things in common, like baseball. But on the issue of the break-up, she sided with me, and as my best friend she was willing to support me in my long-overdue retaliation and hour of need.

Mary Catherine and I took our time. No dogs and no cops were anywhere near the dark alley where I had parked. We did not speak. I got all of the frozen juice cans out of the car, which by this time, had started to thaw nicely since they had now been out of the store's freezer for several hours. We methodically peeled the top off of each can, and then watched the contents escape slowly, like poop glopping over the car's windows—all of them—and especially the windshield. As an added touch, I left one of the cans on top of the hood as a sort of ornament. It was the perfect memento. We threw toilet paper into some of the trees in the backyard for good measure as a sort of postprandial nightcap after an extremely satisfying meal. It was a job well done.

But then there was the loud VW again. The little engine revved into life, and the stupid car pop-popped and bang-banged all the way as I drove out of the alley in reverse. We were both ridiculously ducking our heads down as far inside the car as possible. I was barely able to see behind me as the seemingly self-propelled VW now approached the street. I did a K-turn, and we drove around the end of the block to the main drag, which was Robbie's street. We peered inside his house as we made our way down the street. Lights were on, but there wasn't any movement inside. The family seemed to be watching TV together. I kept going, not believing that they didn't hear us and thanking God profusely.

Mary Catherine finally spoke, "Do you have to drive so fast?"

I looked down at the speedometer.

"I'm only going twenty-five miles an hour," I replied. That was well within speed limit. In fact, it *was* the speed limit.

"Oh."

I took Mary Catherine back to her house on the other side of town, pop-popping and bang-banging all the way, then began the return trip home where my arrival was of course, pre-announced by the car at least three blocks before I ever turned onto Yellow Rose Lane. The noisy, little car heralded great loads of bad karma as I approached the house because Mom and Dad very angrily greeted me on the front porch. It was about 11:00 p.m., and the porch light was off. I saw in the shadows that Dad had started to take off his belt, and I thought he was going to make me pull down my pants, which would have been more humiliating to me at age sixteen than the belt itself. Instead, they asked me what I had been doing, and I told them the truth: Mary Catherine and I had gone tee peeing. I didn't mention the juice on Robbie's car. Tee peeing seemed to wrap it up pretty succinctly. It was the truth, and the truth set me free.

Dad immediately burst into laughter, then presented a most shocking confession, "I remember one time I took and pooped in a paper bag, set 'er on fire and threw it on someone's front porch. You're okay, Kelly, I don't care what everybody else says about you." He led the way inside the house while I followed behind mutely, not believing my luck, and thanking God profusely for the second time that evening. Then both he and Mom started venting about Mary Catherine's parents and the very frosty reception they'd received when they had telephoned the Josephson residence to see if they knew where I was. The Josephsons' reaction was to let Mom and Dad know how very rude it was to receive calls after 9:30 p.m. Mom and Dad were heartily offended, and the rest of the earful I got that evening was directed at Mr. and Mrs. Josephson; God bless them both.

Of course, in the ensuing days, Mary Catherine and I made sure to keep our faces straight whenever Robbie would talk about the injustice done to his car. It was quite the talk of the town. "And they left one of the cans on the hood!" he would say whenever he recalled it. Funny thing, I ran into Robbie at a high school reunion a few years ago. He brought up the frozen juice on his car again. Evidently the special hood ornament still struck a nerve because he mentioned that again, too. Mary Catherine and I did not dare look at each other. Even though their friendship has lasted all of these years, Mary Catherine has never told Robbie that she knows who fouled his car, and, of course, neither have I. It is a secret that we will both take to our graves.

CHAPTER TEN

WEDNESDAY

It's the Wednesday after the great bathroom cleanup, and it's Dad's turn to spend the day with me while Mom works. I arrived early wearing the same work jeans I'd worn all week, along with an old shirt and my red bandanna to keep my hair from getting filthy as I cleaned.

Dad worked the Jumble puzzle in the newspaper while I got started on the sofa again. He asked me to move a huge box that was between the sofa and the wall system. It wasn't heavy, and when I asked about it, he said it contained a lamp that one of Mom's siblings had sent. "I wish they wouldn't do that. They know we don't have room for this stuff!" I looked for a place to put it, and there was literally no place in the living room. I took it down the hall to the first door that would open—Allison's old room—and wiggled it in the room. The door wouldn't open all the way because there was too much stuff in her room, too. I shoved it in as far as I could, then I went back into the living room and relaxed a little bit, Killer in my arms. I kept watching Dad as he slept in his chair, the ever-present little bird's chest scaring me with its deep and uncertain breaths.

Dad didn't like the stationary bicycle that took up the space behind his chair. Mom had bought him that for Father's Day one year, thinking that if he would just exercise, it would help his lungs. But his lungs were way beyond exercise-induced repair and so it sat, the unused, mint-conditioned, recumbent bicycle, acting now as Dad's closet. At least he knew where his clothes were. His shirts hung from the handlebars, and his shorts were draped over the seat. He asked me to take the bike outside and put it out on the deck. He said he didn't think Mom would even notice. But I had my doubts. After the great bathroom cleanup, she'd noticed immediately that a tiny basket had been missing out of all the junk on the stairs and hallway. But I did as he asked and hauled the bike out onto the deck, disturbing the cats as they basked in the afternoon sun. When I came back in, I moved his clothes on top of two boxes that had been squeezed between the bike and whatever other stuff was in the vicinity.

I noticed as I sat down again that the place was beginning to feel cozy to me. There were many things to look at, and I got a weird sort of reassurance in knowing that there was a ton of stuff behind me, protecting my back. Odd. I wondered if my feeling of coziness had to do with the sense of being comforted or protected by the angels. Lots and lots of angels. Was I beginning to feel the same way Mom did? Was that why she noticed when something was gone? Everything, all the comfort behind and before her, was memorized?

Dad was getting into the spirit of things and ordered new gravel for the driveway. He'd decided that we might as well try to make the outside look nice. In fact, that might be easier than the unending gathering, sorting, and tossing I was attempting inside.

For lunch we went for a little drive all the way to Jasper, well west of the farm, and ate at a little Mexican place. The food was great, and Dad paid with cash this time. It's a larger town than the little village of New Haven where we'd lunched on Monday, and some merchants in Jasper were shy about accepting checks. Just down the street was a florist, and I went inside the shop to see if they had any dried eucalyptus. I'd heard that it would keep spiders away. I was sick and tired of finding spider webs in the house. I was also hoping that the eucalyptus would help mask the stink in the house. I bought all that they had—five large boxes full—and spent $70. My purchase made the florist's day.

After that, we decided to run to Walmart. For as much as Mom hates Walmart ("because you have to go ziggy-zaggy and up a hill"), Dad is exactly the opposite. He likes being able to drive around in the store's little scooter since he can't walk all over the place. I'd wanted to buy some baskets for his desk area, and some big, plastic tubs to help organize some of the things in the entry. I went down one aisle, and Dad realized he was going to have to turn the scooter around in order to stay with me. He put it in reverse without looking and nearly plowed into a lady in the dairy section.

We continued on together and went to the pet section. I chose a little cat house for Killer that was like a little hassock covered in carpet but open with a couple of little round "windows" and a ball hanging from its ceiling. Adorable.

Next, we went to the storage section, and I got several big, plastic tubs. I thought I could use those to help Mom store some of her important stuff in the entry and make it look like a proper foyer. I found a few other things for the house, and we headed back home. Dad was still a reliable driver, but I was ever prepared to take the wheel if I needed to. It was a clear day with bright sunshine, the type of day that makes you feel energetic. I thought I could tackle the great cleanup again when we got back to the farm.

Killer got acquainted with his little house, and Dad sat in his chair while I started sifting through the detritus on the sofa. There were many newspapers interspersed with little piles of rubber-banded together letters, bills, and envelopes. Outside each little rubber-banded package were pencil notations. As I sifted through the stuff, I unwrapped every single one and asked Dad about the contents of each envelope. I could have just packed everything up into about twenty garbage bags and be done with it, but I didn't want to throw anything out that might be important, so we both became slaves to the tedious process.

Dad was a very willing accomplice. There were newspapers from twenty years ago. Entire newspapers were saved, but the pertinent news was usually only a tiny portion of one page, devoted to the accomplishment of one of the grandkids, usually accompanied by a little photograph. What was it with the stacks and stacks of newspapers? Why not just clip out the meaningful story? Or did all of it have meaning to her? I'd done a little research of my own regarding hoarding when we were at the library the other day, and I had used one of the public computers to do some internet searches. According to one source, *www.ocfoundation.org*, one of the factors in OCD-based hoarding is an obsession, for instance, a superstition that throwing something away might result in something bad happening. So what was it that Mom was afraid would happen? Was she afraid something would happen to the grandkids if she threw the entire newspaper away?

The website *www.ocfoundation.org* also stated that traumatic events were common in hoarders. Stressful events might also have to do with periods of more aggressive hoarding. There was also a reference to hoarding behavior occurring in adolescence. There seemed to be three stressful life events in my mother's case: the deaths of two sons, and the move to a house she hated. I could not think of anything I'd ever heard of in her childhood that could have triggered her hoarding behavior as a young adolescent. In fact, the more I thought about it, the more I felt with certainty that we could rule that out. Mom had had a wonderful childhood. In fact, I'd often wished that my grandmother had been my mom instead of my own mother. In any event, the affliction in Mother's case seemed to be the result of some sort of loss.

I got through the envelopes, and Dad decided to take a little nap. I continued working and found a couple of Christmas presents I recognized that I'd given them a few years before. They'd been unwrapped and left on the sofa, unused. I picked them up and put them over by my handbag. I figured I might as well get some use out of them since the folks didn't have any interest. I doubted they would even miss them. I also found some plastic pink ponies inside an old-fashioned doll case, and a little pot of plastic forget-me-nots.

These discoveries reminded of a game we used to play as kids called "Dr. Quack." This was a card game of sorts. There was a script that was read, and at certain points in the story, a blank, underlined space in the script would indicate that the reader was to let one of the other players fill the space with a word or series of words as indicated on the card that they would draw from a pile. It went something like this:

"Let's have some fun today! We'll all play Dr. Quack! But when you've finished with the game, please put the cards all back. Dr. Quack is very wise. It's all great fun, agreed? If you have an ailment, he'll make it right. Just have some faith. You'll see. You say you have an ailing back? He'll fix it quick, that Dr. Quack! Dr. Quack is very quick. He'll make a remedy so slick. Or if a tummy ache's your plight, he'll fix that, too, and make it right! Any ailment, large or small, Quack will fix them—fix them all.

"Dr. Quack is a nice old man with *four blue toadstools* on his back. He wears *a bunch of pansies* on his hat. His shirt is made of *hot boiling oil*. So very wise is Dr. Quack. He walks around with *a fresh apple pie* and in his pocket is *a hard green tomato*. He carries with him *your uncle John's toupee* and holds that together with *a piece of bailing wire, a bridal veil, five cute puppies, a rotten egg,* and two pieces of *some purple petunias.* Dr. Quack will never lack. His cane is made of *a bowlful of happiness,* and his vest is made of *two steel bolts* and *your aunt Maisie's headwrap.* His trousers are made of *your father's newspaper.* He will not slack, will Dr. Quack. He has it all, does Dr. Quack. He has *your mother's nose* and *a tree full of kittens* to help him on his way. You say you have a stomachache? He'll make a special remedy to make your day. So step right up and see what the good doctor will say. Take *three horned toads* and mix that with *your grandmother's smelling salts.* Pour in *an old brown shoe,* sprinkle with *a seven-layered cake,* and heat until ready. Or what about your aching back? Quack has a remedy for that! Pick up *a pair of suspenders* from *a thimbleful of sunshine,* take *a Costa Rican monarch butterfly* and mix that with *your dresser drawers.* Stir carefully with three scoops of *an old bicycle pump,* add *some smelly fish, a cast iron skillet, your grandpa's long johns* and three slices of *a bunch of pretty forget-me-nots.* Stir with *your monkey's uncle* until done and top with *four pink ponies.* See? Don't you feel better now? Let's play the game again. Just shuffle the cards and pick a new reader."

Of course, the story would change with each reading, depending on which cards were drawn.

By the end of the day, Killer had become well acquainted with his little house, and I had cleared away enough stuff so that I could actually see the fabric on the back of the sofa. Dad's eyes teared when he woke up from his nap and saw that a bit of the sofa was visible once again. "Come sit down, Kelly, and take a break!" I walked over and hugged him, and both of us started crying. It seemed weird standing there, hugging my dad. He'd never hugged us when we were kids. I looked behind him and for the first time, noticed some winter clothes that must have been in one of the piles all along. He asked me if I would wash them at Reese's for him. Mom could no longer get to the laundry room, and they'd been washing all of their clothes out by hand in the sink.

I'd filled quite a number of bags full of trash and hauled them downstairs so we could take them back to Reese's house before Mom got home. We were very careful not to let Mom see the bags we were taking away because we knew she'd want to go through the trash to see what was being pitched and whether it was salvageable.

I remembered one time during my summer break as a freshman in college that I'd gone through some boxes labeled as mine and had started tossing a few items. One of those in particular was an orange wax harmonica with a black skeleton on it that was intended to be a chewable treat. It smelled sweet and was one of those old Halloween things you would see at that time of year. I'd won that at a school party in the fourth grade. We were playing a game similar to "Pin the Tail on the Donkey" except that this was "Pin the Nose on the Jack-O-Lantern."

I'd cheated and won. I had tilted my head back so I could look beneath the blindfold and was able to see exactly the spot to put the nose on that jack-o-lantern. It had brought me no joy, my ill-gotten gain. I almost told the teachers I had cheated but then realized they probably already knew, and had decided not to call me on it out of sympathy over baby Stephen's death a few months before then.

But this object had haunted me all those years, and I had finally decided to rid my life of it. Then Mother came into the room, went through my trash, and made me rethink every single object that I was throwing out. I ended up disposing of two or three items out of about twenty-five. Unfortunately, the wax harmonica did not make its way into the trash and it lurks even now in some silent location, waiting to remind me of my dishonesty when I discover it again.

I felt spent now, just like the day Mom had insisted on going through my trash. It had taken some doing on my part to get to the point where I myself felt that I could throw something away; I had become used to hanging onto things, just like Mother. I could certainly understand why she had been so upset earlier in the week.

The exhaustion was now part of me like some disease I could not shake. Along with the emotional stress of seeing Dad like he was, there was the fatigue of cleaning and the anxiety of trying to hide the results. That night I dreamed of cobwebs and envelopes that kept reappearing no matter how many times I removed them. Had I ever worked so hard before? Yes.

CHAPTER ELEVEN
THE VALUE OF HARD WORK

The wake-up call came at 2:00 a.m. I should be used to it by now, but it was still tough after working thirteen hours the previous day. "Get awake, Kelly! Allison, Reese, get awake!" It was never "Wake up!" It was always, "Get awake," the hard "g" sound lending additional emphasis.

Grandma had opened the Shiloh Café and Grill and had also taken over the doughnut shop next door, which she'd named Cock-a-Doodle Doughnuts, or sometimes, just "Doodle" for short when answering the phone. When we answered the phone as "Doodle!" people knew that they'd reached the doughnut shop. Sometimes when Grandma answered the phone I thought she sounded exactly like a rooster.

When we answered the phone in the restaurant, though, we had to carefully articulate "Shiloh Café and Grill" because there was a Hi-Lo Auto Repair and Body Parts shop a few blocks away, and their phone number was the same as the restaurant's, but off by one number. Sometimes we got calls from people who thought they'd reached the auto repair shop, and we'd say, "This is the Shiloh Café and Grill. You want Hi-Lo Auto Repair and Body Parts, but please do come in and visit us for a cup of coffee or a bite to eat while you wait for your vehicle to be serviced!"

Grandma had to start the doughnuts by 2:30 a.m. in order to have them ready when the store opened at 5:30 a.m. The restaurant opened at 7:00 a.m. and closed at 8:00 p.m. I don't think she ever slept. After we would close up the restaurant, we'd go back to the house and try to be in bed by 10:00 p.m. We'd always eaten dinner at the restaurant, so there was no need to prepare a meal when we got home. Grandma did the laundry every night, and when I would get up at 2:00 a.m., my white waitress uniform would be waiting for me, clean and freshly pressed.

We weren't really needed in the wee hours of doughnut making. But I think Grandma didn't want to run back and forth between the house and the businesses because we had a twenty-minute commute from the house into the little town. "The early bird catches the worm!" she'd say. So, she'd haul us out of the house, and we'd all bed down on cots or tables in the back room of the doughnut shop until time to get up and get ready to work in the restaurant. I was never able to go back to sleep after the early wake-up call, but at least it was a little rest before having to get up and be on my feet all day.

The little restaurant and doughnut shop were situated in the building that she owned in the little downtown area. The establishments were mirror images, each with a single large window and door at the front, and with the length of the building running all the way to the alley that bisected the block. It was a long, narrow, two-story, red brick building, with many warrens in the back and a maze-like hallway from one business to the other. Sometimes it seemed like it was just too much hassle to try to go from one business to the other in the back of the building. Oftentimes, we would just go out the front door and enter the front door from one business to the other.

The front entrances were set at angles facing each other in the style of small-town buildings from the 1920s. The business on the left, the restaurant, had its entrance angled toward the doughnut shop, and likewise, the doughnut shop had its entrance angled toward the restaurant. Both businesses were adorned with window boxes, which, during the summer months, held a rebellion of trailing geraniums and ivy. This year Grandma had chosen reds, oranges, and fuchsia pinks, guaranteed to draw customers in.

The restaurant didn't have a window display beyond its little window box; only seating was visible, but the doughnut shop had a tasty display that changed daily and was always fresh. The one constant in the display was a big, round rooster head glazed doughnut (minus the hole), like it was destined to be a giant filled doughnut. Grandma had figured out how to make a doughnut about twelve inches across. She fashioned a cockscomb and beak, fried it, turned it in the huge vat somehow without getting grease all over the place, and then glazed it just like a proper glazed doughnut. Each day she would put a little different twist on it. People kept asking if they could buy the big rooster head doughnut, but it was never for sale. Sometimes the cockscomb was a series of big loopy finger-like extensions, much like the type of thing one sees at Thanksgiving when schoolchildren bring home artwork they have fashioned by tracing their hands. Other times the cockscomb was a short series of nubs, looking rather emasculated, which made me wonder if Grandma had recently had trouble with a man. Probably one of her suppliers, I would think.

At one time, the doughnut shop had been the home of Virginia's Gifts, where all the young brides in town registered their china. But Virginia had long since retired, and Grandma had been happy with the new tenant—the original doughnut shop owners—as long as they paid their rent. They'd built up the business, then decided they could no longer tolerate the long hours, so they sold the business to Grandma.

The restaurant was decorated in appetizing greens. Green was Grandma's favorite color. The booths were a nice shade of dark green. There were three booths. On the right side of the establishment were four tables in an early American style. She'd intended to have a little seating area with barstools at the grill, but due to space limitations, she'd had to abandon that idea. It would have been nice to have the extra seats because it would have meant additional income.

The doughnut shop was sparsely furnished. There was a simple cabinet in front with three sections set at angles to each other, the broadest facing and parallel to the door. People would be lined up twelve deep in there at 5:30 a.m. One lady always bought a dozen glazed doughnuts. She told me she could no longer tolerate the blueberry ones because she had eaten an entire dozen of blueberry doughnuts in one sitting a few months back, and it made her so sick she couldn't stomach the thought. I'm not sure if she ever ate a dozen glazed doughnuts all at once or not. If she did, it didn't make her sick because she came in every few days for more doughnuts as her ample figure testified.

The businesses were directly across the street from the town's tiny bus station, and the very spot where I had seen Jared kiss Anna for what I was certain would be the last time. Given the proximity to the station, one might think that this would have generated a lot of extra business for the local establishments. But given that there were only six or so busses that came into town each day—three eastbound: morning, midday, and evening, and three westbound: morning, midday, and evening—there wasn't that much additional activity, and so Grandma relied on repeat, local customers.

But the setting of the businesses was pleasant and not far away from other major draws. This was on a little stretch of Petunia Street, just a few blocks west of the local bank, three family-owned pharmacies that had soda fountains and lots of toiletries, and the post office. There was a dry goods store just down the street that smelled of old-lady perfumes and new fabric. They also sold women's undergarments, and Grandma bought a couple of bras for me there. Across from the dry goods store was Dora's Variety Five and Dime Store. You could find all sorts of interesting little things in that store. Dora's had everything from school supplies to small leather goods to beauty products, and they even had a little cafeteria area with a soda fountain to compete with the ones in the little drugstores. Dora's had the best hot fudge sundaes. We didn't serve those at the restaurant. Up the street the town became quickly residential, and this was the better part of the town. Kids who lived in this area went to prestigious MacPherson Elementary School.

I'd haul myself out of bed and throw on some clothes. I never bothered to put on the waitress uniform until it was time for my shift. Once we got to the doughnut shop, we'd try to go to sleep, but it was difficult because Grandma was always talking. Another lady worked the early shift at the doughnut shop alongside Grandma, and there was usually laughter because Grandma was the world's best unknown comedienne. She would have been a great broadcast journalist, too, because she was never at a loss for words, quick on her feet, and asked great questions. Sometimes she would ask things that I thought weren't really appropriate. I might tell her that the situation wasn't any of our business, and she would say something like, "It *was* my business, because I asked!"

I found myself becoming interested in the comings and goings of the customers. Some very interesting characters frequented the businesses. It was easier to people-watch in the restaurant because the patrons were there longer. On the doughnut side, it was just a quick in-and-out. But given that ours was a little tourist town, there were some interesting people who patronized the doughnut shop, too. Sometimes they would be from a place like Minnesota or North Dakota and speak with very charming accents, and they would ask for things I'd never heard of, like éclairs.

On occasion, a boy I had a crush on would come into the restaurant. Unfortunately, I could never think of anything cute to say when I took his order, so he would just eat and then leave. And sometimes, there were boys who came in who made me uncomfortable. There was one guy in particular who was about six-foot-eight-inches tall and had hit his head one time too many. He would always order a "Seb'n Up" and sit there and stare at me while I went about my business. Grandma took me aside and told me not to mind him. He was a little off and wouldn't be any harm. He always came in with his father, who would sit and stare too. I wondered if he was a little off as well.

And there was another man who would come in during the week for morning and afternoon coffee. He was very nice and worked in the bank as a loan officer. He was always well dressed, but there was something very interesting about this man and that was that he had unusual eyes. One eye was blue, and the other one was brown. I sometimes found them so interesting that I would realize I had been staring at them. I didn't want to be rude, so I tried to avoid looking him straight in the eye. I would look at the table while I served his coffee instead of at him. One day, Allison went over to him and said loud enough for the entire restaurant to hear, "Did you know that you have one blue eye and one brown eye?"

This nice gentleman answered very graciously, "Why, yes, I did! They have been that way ever since I was born." Golly, she had some nerve, and Grandma nearly died of embarrassment because this guy was her loan officer at the bank and was also one of the important, local, repeat customers.

Sometimes when Grandma would leave the restaurant to run an errand, she would leave me in charge of the grill. Normally she and Ramona shared the grill. I'm not sure where Ramona was that day, but I was in charge of the grill for the first time and absolutely petrified that someone would come in and want to place a grill order. But my fear summoned the inevitable, and before I knew it, Reggie Dover came into the restaurant and wanted bacon and eggs, over-easy. Reggie Dover was a member of the only African-American family in town. They ran a little convenience store on the poor side of town. Reggie was married to an Italian lady named Maria, and they had a little son together. Reggie had met Maria when he was stationed in Italy during World War II.

Grandma hired Maria to work in the doughnut shop and had told me that if Reggie Dover ever came in the restaurant, we were never to charge him for his meal. The Dovers had been good to Grandma and had let her buy food on credit when times were tough. I was a terrible cook, and the food looked so bad I was embarrassed to serve him. The bacon was nice and crispy; it was hard to mess up the toast, but the over-easy eggs could have used a few more practice runs. That was one occasion where I felt that "on the house" was justified for sure. But he insisted on paying and didn't complain about my cooking.

Grandma served fresh-baked pies every day. She usually had seven choices: three cream pies (usually banana, coconut cream, and chocolate) and four fruit pies (usually cherry, apple, peach, and a berry pie, like blueberry or blackberry, or sometimes strawberry-rhubarb). The pie lady would come in around 9:00 a.m. with her pies. She'd been up since the wee hours as well, baking her pies. She had a handy-looking contraption to carry all of the pies in without disturbing them. It was a tiered wire design of some sort. Not the type of thing you would find in one of the local stores. Clearly, this was a professional pie-baker.

I thought it was nice that Grandma patronized the locals and that the locals patronized her. Farmers would come into town on a Saturday and eat at the restaurant or buy doughnuts. The weekday coffee rush was nonexistent on Saturdays, but there was other business coming in the door. I observed that the little town tried to take care of its own people, just by the locals doing business in a kind sort of way and helping each other.

Sunday was our day off. Both businesses were closed, but Grandma used that day to catch up on her garden, do any canning if necessary, and clean the house. Mom would come to get us on Saturday night, and we'd spend Sunday at our own house. Mom sometimes helped in the restaurant, but she was mainly busy coffee klatching with the neighbors in our own little town from about 9:00 a.m. until right before lunchtime and doing yet another redecorating project on the house. She was happiest in the new town with the house she loved. And whereas she may have felt that she ought to help her mother more often, she didn't feel compelled enough to make it a regular habit. When Mother came to pick us up, she would haul back what seemed like tons of day-old doughnuts. They filled the freezer and began taking over our deep freeze. Mother could never stand to throw away any type of food, but after working all week in Cock-a-Doodle Doughnuts, the thought of actually eating a Cock-a-Doodle doughnut was repulsive, and so they multiplied in our freezers.

Extra cash was kept in a large, old, rectangular gold-faced tin in the back room, stored in an unobtrusive place among some sacks of doughnut flour underneath an old table that sometimes doubled as a bed for us. The piled sacks comprised the only clutter in the entire building. Even so, they were arranged very neatly. When someone would come in with a large bill, like a $50 or $100 bill, the person on duty would run excitedly in the back and tell Grandma that they needed change. Grandma would get the tin out and sift through the money. We were never robbed at the businesses, and Grandma was never robbed on her way to the bank. She'd say, "If somebody comes in with a gun and wants money, just give it to 'em." She always carried a large shoulder bag, and on days when she went to the bank with a large deposit, she'd carry the bag tightly under her arm but tried to look nonchalant, as if she weren't carrying a large wad of cash, but was just out for a stroll around the block.

When she came back from the bank she would usually "do the books." We stayed out of her way because it was her least favorite thing to do. She had an old ledger book and would often become frustrated with herself because she had a habit of reversing figures. For instance, $87.68 would become $86.78. That would mess with your mind after a bit, and she'd be a little cranky. Usually she was in good humor, though, unless she was doing the books or one of us was chewing gum. It wasn't the gum chewing per se that bothered her; it was when one of the gum wrappers would fly into the fan that was perched at the table where the staff sat. She detested clutter of any sort in either of her establishments; it was simply not allowed. "I told you not to chew that sour stink gum in here!" (Now, instead of the word, "stink," you need to think about a four-letter word beginning with the same letter. By golly, she could talk like a sailor.) Adams Sour Stripe gums were all the rage back then and easily affordable. My favorite was sour lime.

We worked for tips, mainly. I was supposed to get paid an hourly wage, but I was on "Granddaughter Wages" and had agreed to let Grandma pay me what she owed me in a few years when I went to college. In the meantime, I was happy to work for tips like Allison and Reese, who bused and washed the dishes in the restaurant. On occasion, we'd get enough saved up and would take a little shopping trip down the street. One day, Reese and I went into Dora's Variety Five and Dime Store and were admiring some little hair bands, pins, and wallets. I'd purchased a lovely lavender wallet there recently. It had a faux diamond-crusted French poodle on the front cover, and I was interested in adding another piece to my vast collection.

Suddenly a man appeared out of the back and demanded that Reese take out the thing that she'd put in her purse. Reese looked at him, dumbfounded.

"She didn't put anything in her purse," I said, still in my waitress uniform, adopting the role of self-appointed upstanding citizen and authority on the situation. "Well, it looked like she did. You girls need to leave the store now."

We ran back to the restaurant in tears and spilled out the story to Grandma. She marched all ninety-eight pounds of her red-haired self down the street and gave them what-for. She told them that we were honest girls, and just looking. We might have even purchased something if they hadn't asked us to leave. She told them that we wouldn't have done anything like that. Evidently the way we were positioned, and in a pair, led them to believe that we were up to no good. These people seemed to think that shoplifting was typically done exactly the way we were browsing.

And even though many years have passed, Reese and I look back on that time with gratitude. It was a reassuring and very necessary thing for a child to have an adult who would be a reliable advocate for them. Someone you could count on, who would handle a thing and report back to you. Unfortunately, this was something that our own mother was almost never able to do for us. Her own perpetual victimization always got in the way.

There was one time, however, when Mom really went to bat for me. I was about ten or eleven years old and was riding my bike back from an errand at the little local grocery when two teenage boys known to be troublemakers were also riding their bikes and tried to run me off mine. There was a wooded area nearby, and they were trying to force me in there. I peddled my bike as hard as I could down a back alley. I knew the alley well and ducked every pothole. They eventually gave up, but I ran screaming into the house. Mom called the police. I spent one humiliating afternoon in the back of a police car trying to identify one of the boys and his bike. That was the only time Mom stepped up to the plate: it was when my physical safety was at risk. All the other times—like when I was supposed to be on the principal's honor roll at school and had been left off the list—she seemed entirely powerless to do anything.

But Grandma demonstrated that she could be our advocate—someone we could count on. Reese and I loved her for that. And with a mother like that—our Grandma—why had our own mother never been able to stand up for herself? Life was an odd thing sometimes.

CHAPTER TWELVE
THE TRUTH REVEALED

Grandma was the original reporter. She would report things about people that I'm sure they would have preferred not be reported. And she would report things about *you* that you definitely would prefer not to be reported. Some of these revelations were made publicly, in your presence: "Reese, are you menstruating? Is that is why your face is broken out, or do you have acne?" (Spoken loudly in the little cafeteria at Dora's Variety Five and Dime Store during a Sunday break from the restaurant.) Or, in her house, when a cute neighbor came to visit: "Kelly and Fred will sit here at the table and look at each other, while I go bring us something to eat! Kelly, tell Fred that you're a straight-A student!" This wasn't true, but it was true in Grandma's mind.

The restaurant was very fertile territory for Grandma's reporting capabilities. If she wasn't reporting something to one of the patrons about somebody else, she was reporting something to us about the so-and-so who had just come in and left.

One day Grandma was chitchatting as usual. She was saying, "Eeee! If I'd known Mrs. Barron's little granddaughter was about to die, I'd have just let that child have that hairbrush she wanted. Grandma doesn't think straight sometimes! Kelly, did you pluck your eyebrows? They look very nice. Reese! SSI! Stick Stomach In!" Reese immediately sat up straight and sucked in her gut. Grandma also had a problem with the way Reese walked, which was more like clomping or stomping, but because Reese wasn't walking at that moment, Grandma couldn't say anything about that. Her modus operandi was to catch the person in the act of whatever it was that needed correcting.

"Lacy told me that Joe got a $50 check in the mail when one of his cancer patients died. The patient was an old man from a poor family, and he had told his family to send something to that nice doctor once he was gone. Joe just flung himself down on the bed and cried and cried when he got that letter! Yes, I would have just given that child that hairbrush. Kelly, would you please take your young legs to the back room and bring me that big ice bucket?"

I left to run the errand, which took a little bit of time because I couldn't find where someone had last put the big ice bucket Grandma wanted, even though the back room was very organized, with no clutter except the doughnut flour sacks. When I came back, Grandma was still talking, "I had a letter from Marie! You remember, Marie Gustafson!" Of course I remembered Marie Gustafson. She was the angel who had cleaned our house when little Stephen was born. She was also Warren's mother and Grandma's best friend.

"Marie, Roger and Warren will be stopping by!" Oh, God. Warren. I hadn't seen him in about five years. My heart skipped a beat, and I felt weak at the knees. Hunk-a-Hunk-a-Burnin'-Love was going to be visiting the restaurant!

I handed the ice bucket to Grandma. "Thank you, honey. They are moving back to the Midwest from the East Coast!" There were no patrons in the restaurant just then, only us. I went over to the table where Reese and Allison were and sat down as quickly as I could before my knees gave out.

"Wheee! Kelly will see Warren again!"

That last statement immediately prompted Allison and Reese to take action:

"Kelly and Warren, sitting in a tree—
K-i-s-s-i-n-g!
First comes love—
Then comes marriage—
Then comes Warren with the baby carriage!"

"Oh, stuff a sock in it!" I told them angrily. They were probably the most annoying things on the planet, considering of course, the very possible exception: Mr. Inertia Man himself, Barry Dooley.

"Hush!" Grandma said. What if a customer comes in here and hears you girls acting that way!"

Grandma wiped her hands on her apron, glanced at her watch and then turned to me, "Eeeee! It's 4:30, Kelly. Would you please go next door and help Maria clean up the doughnut shop so we can get ready to close?"

"Sure, Grandma!" I had always liked working on the doughnut side. There were the few pans at the end of the day to clean up, but it wasn't nearly as much work to close as the restaurant was.

This had been a good day. There was only one-half of a pan of glazed doughnuts left. I knew they would be tasteless and stale the next day, but that wouldn't prevent Mother from taking them home and rearranging one of the freezers to find space for them. This was Saturday and she'd be along shortly to take us and the valuable doughnuts home.

One day Grandma was entertaining us as usual when we were driving back out to her house at the end of a long day. Whenever Grandma drove, she would move her thumbs back and forth across the steering wheel as if they were miniature windshield wipers. Her painted nails were always fascinating to watch, and she was doing it again today.

Suddenly she grabbed her chest. "Now, Kelly, if Grandma is driving down the street and she all of a sudden can't drive the car, you just reach over and turn the key off." A remark like that would certainly get your attention.

A few weeks later she had a heart attack and was hospitalized.

After she recovered, Grandma sold her house and asked her tenant to move out of the other little house she still owned, so she could move back into it. Grandma then sold many of her possessions to generate cash in order to retire. One of the items she made sure to keep was a beautiful, little antique quilt that her aunt had made. I'd always liked using it when I slept over, and Grandma had always pulled it out of the closet for me. It was a twin-sized quilt in a "log cabin" pattern with a red border that was so old and faded that the fabric had taken on a rose color. Some of the stitching was loose, and some of the fabric had worn thin, but I loved it.

We liked Grandma's little old house that was now new to us again. It was sort of run down and comfy. There was always the smell of food, wood polish, and old linens. There may have been little stacks of things here and there, such as her beloved paperback books, mostly Zane Grey and Louis L'Amour titles, but they were orderly and tidy. She could no longer run the restaurant business or doughnut shop and had sold them, but I still came over to see her frequently, and it was easier now that I could drive. She had made herself a little garden and got a dog she called "Tiger" for protection. He was a good barker. I came over on one occasion, and she made me a Spam sandwich, and we had fresh cherry and yellow plum tomatoes from her garden. We were having a little picnic of sorts at a card table we'd moved into the yard for the occasion. And over that lunch, she reported something to me that I had suspected but hadn't really wanted to have confirmed.

My parents had married in the month of July. I was born the following January. That does not add up to the nine months, which I had learned in Biology class, was the necessary gestation period for a human being. I didn't want to know, but she told me that I had been conceived in the backseat of a car in the very driveway that she was now sweeping her arm toward. And she sounded so upset about it that I started crying. I cried for my mother for being so young and not finishing high school, and I cried for my dad because I knew Grandma had hated him because they'd had to get married, and I cried for myself for being the product of all that sadness and disappointment. And I cried generally because my mother seemed so inept and dependent and without a shred of backbone, and I cried because I really didn't like her very much, and that made me cry because I felt badly about *that*.

Grandma continued, "I told your father to let her finish school! Your mother had always been a marvelous student, and loved reading. I noticed she began reading more and more when she was about ten years old. She would say that she was going to escape into a book in her room, and escape she did. Did you know she began her book collection about that time? Eeeee! It was as if she wanted to remove herself from her normal life. Books, books, and more books. Then your father came along and everything changed."

She shook her head as if to rid herself of the bad memory, but Grandma didn't stop there. She was in the mood to report. She also told me that Mother would have stood up to Dad the evening of the great egg, toilet paper, and frozen juice caper. Grandma assured me that Mom would not have allowed Dad to make me pull down my pants or strike me with his belt. I couldn't believe that Mom would ever have grown a pair and stood up to Dad if I hadn't actually observed that very phenomenon on the day Dad had smacked

Reese when he was trying to listen to Paul Harvey, and she had started choking on a cherry tomato. So maybe when it had to do with a physical threat, Mom had the ability to advocate for her children.

Then Grandma started talking about my little brother, Jason. He was born when I was just a toddler; we were thirteen months apart. Jason died when he was six weeks old from SIDS. She'd received the news from my father who had had to drive clear across the little town from where we were living to go over to Grandma's to use her telephone. Mom and Dad had been too poor to afford one of their own. He rushed up to the door and began knocking loudly. Grandma opened the wooden front door, but the screen door was still locked. It had an old-fashioned lock on it, the hook type, and because Dad was grabbing the door trying to open it, she couldn't get it unlocked. They started arguing about getting the door open, and in frustration Dad finally said through the screen, "Let me in, I have to call the police. Jason is dead!"

She looked at me, tears in her eyes. "Here we were, arguing about the door and little Jason was dead. It was that very front door, right over there! Eeeee! Wasn't that a horrible way for me to treat your father?"

The police came and went. But as they left they said to my mother, "What could you have done to prevent this from happening?" What indeed? She was standing there at the top of the stairs, breasts heavy with milk and empty arms. Little Jason had slept through the night for the first time. Because he had slept through his normal feeding, Mother wanted Dad to bring him to her so she could nurse him. She was leaking milk. Dad went into Jason's room and called out, "He's dead!"

Mother had yelled at him, "Don't you lie to me! What a cruel joke! Bring my baby to me!"

Dad brought little Jason to her. He had found his little son, a horrible shade of blue, lying in the bassinet with his little fist pushed toward his face, as if he had tried to help himself breathe.

"Eeeee! Grandma is feeling blue today!"

Well, thanks, Grandma. Now I was, too. I cried the entire thirty-mile trip back home in my little Volkswagen, the hot August prairie wind pushing the car sideways so strongly that I had to roll two windows down a little bit just to keep the car from going off the road. I'd known about little Jason—in fact, my parents had asked me if I remembered anything about him— but I hadn't known about all that.

I was glad to put that summer behind me. School was starting again. The leaves would be changing soon, and it would be Thanksgiving before we knew it, and then Christmas.

That Thanksgiving at Grandma's little old house was one of the most memorable with the traditional turkey, accompanied by Grandma's scalloped oysters and cranberry sauce and mince and pumpkin pies and sweet potatoes and little LeSeuer peas. I could smell everything as soon as I walked in. The little place was just as it always had been. The lazy Susan in the corner of the kitchen that I'd loved to play in was still there. The old wallpaper still clung to the walls, and the hardwood floors were badly scuffed, but the place smelled like love.

Grandma reported on the state of the family to everybody, and we enjoyed the good food and each other's company. And that Thanksgiving, I realized I had something else to be thankful for: a new beginning.

CHAPTER THIRTEEN
A NEW BEGINNING

Over the winter, we continued to see Grandma. She would sometimes drive over to our house and see us after school. We no longer had to compete with Jared's family for her attention; they had moved away. Grandma was pleased that Allison had made a breakthrough with her cleanliness / perfectionism behavior. Grandma herself knew the benefits of counseling quite well as she had been very depressed after Grandpa had died.

Allison spoke very highly of her therapist. She said one thing she had learned was to take just one day at a time. I'd never met her counselor, but she described him as a nice man with wire-rimmed spectacles and graying hair who smiled a lot. And he had an attractive office, which she described as "cheerful."

Allison was very much into interior design at this stage and had decided she wanted to be an interior designer when she grew up. She would regale us over dinner with facts about the color wheel, and which colors complemented others. Allison had critiqued my own decorating scheme in the pink bedroom on several occasions. The strands of bubble gum wrappers just did not go with anything. She would say something like, "You know, Kelly, those gum wrapper strands have way too many colors."

"Yes, but that's exactly why I like them. I love all the colors."

"But they are hanging all over the place, and they don't go with the pink décor. The pink is rather a pale, muted pink, and these colors are too bright. If you really wanted to make a statement, you should do strands only in Adams Sour Lime gum because that green would complement the pink very well. Alternatively, you could do strands only in Wrigley's Doublemint Gum. *That* green would also work. Or, if you wanted to just stick with the pink theme, you could consider using Adams Teaberry wrappers. That rose pink would be wonderful! But the yellow of the Juicy Fruit wrappers, well, it's *actually* more of a *daffodil*, is just too bright."

"Daffodil, marigold, kumquat…"

Allison interrupted me, "Actually, kumquat would be more of a yellow-orange, not yellow."

"Okay, Allison, whatever." I imagined myself rolling my eyes, which was what I really wanted to do. "They are nicely designed just the way they are, and they are most perfectly arranged in an excellent way," I would retort. "Are we done here now?"

She would leave in a huff, presumably to stir up some mischief with Reese.

But I was wise to her. I was pretty sure Allison had wanted me to take the gum wrapper strands down, especially the one over the door, so she could enter my room undetected when I wasn't there. She may have been taller and bossier than me, but I was still the big sister, and it *was* still my room, whether it had her seal of approval or not.

However, she approved of the décor of the therapist's
office. It had been decorated in the "mod" style of the
late 1960s. There was a grand black lacquer coffee
table on which sat a box of tissues and a lovely floral
arrangement, always in bright colors; it changed weekly.
At either end of the rectangular coffee table was a big,
comfy, round chair. One was red and the other one
was yellow-orange, or more accurately, "kumquat." She
usually took the yellow-orange one because she liked
the color, and it was at the far end of the room, facing
the office door. On occasion, she would sit on the
loveseat to the left of the coffee table. It was a bright
floral pattern of big flowers in fuchsias, yellows, oranges
and reds on a white background. She felt comfortable
there; it was smaller than the sofa and just her size.
She never took the grand sofa that faced the loveseat
because it didn't seem quite as inviting, even though
it was very attractive as well. It was covered in a nice
neutral that balanced the bright colors of the other
furnishings. The sofa was filled with a riot of brightly-
colored pillows in various patterns. She said the pillows
seemed to represent other extra people and even though
she might be the only human sitting there, she felt that
it would be crowded, in spite of the expanse of the sofa.
She never took the red chair because that would have
meant her back was to the door. She had a bug-a-boo
about not having her back to a door. I guessed it to be a
remnant of the old boogey man days.

All of these marvelous furnishings sat on pristine,
white, shag, wall-to-wall carpet. I had been easily
able to imagine how beautiful that office was the way

Allison had described it. I could see how she would say it was cheerful.

During one of her last sessions, Allison's therapist acknowledged that our family had been through a lot. He asked her if she thought there was anything useful she could do about her experiences. She had twirled a strand of her dark hair and thought a bit. "Hmm. Well, I suppose I could do something to help other people, just like other people helped us when Stevie died. And I could try to be a better friend, just like when my friends helped me discover that I could eat without using napkins to touch my food at school."

She thought about that idea over the ensuing weeks. What could she do? Decorating was fun but it was expensive. Even though she might want to donate a decorating project or help someone else, everyone's taste was different, and she didn't want to get into arguments with people over colors. After all, she had had enough of that with me. So, she thought about something else that might be fun and would be especially helpful. She concluded that she wanted to volunteer as a candy striper in the local hospital. This was surprising in light of her prior aversion to microorganisms. But candy striper it was; she had turned fourteen and was eligible.

So, she tried it, and discovered that she loved everything about it: the clean hospital smell, the precautions against infection and disease, and providing assistance to others, both hospital staff and patients. She had the mercy gift described in the Bible. Allison was sunshine on steroids and had the ability to make people laugh. She always said that laughter was the best medicine. In addition to the various non-medical volunteer activities that candy stripers do, she also read to little children who had been hospitalized. She would take a supply of books to read to them. One of the books she always brought along with her was our dog-eared, beloved copy of Dr. Seuss' *One Fish, Two Fish, Red Fish, Blue Fish.*

Allison said that helping other people always made her feel better. She encouraged us to do the same. But the reality was that none of us shared quite the same enthusiasm for volunteering. We all had our own stuff we were busy with. This did not matter; we found that Allison was not backing down. She spent many evenings at the dinner table pressing us until we all finally gave in.

Reese decided to give some piano recitals at our little church and pass a hat for donations. She donated all of the proceeds to charity. Half went to the church and half went to March of Dimes. I asked *The Band* to do a free concert and ask for donations. We took in $141.00, quite a princely sum in the late 1960s. (It was exactly the same amount as the monthly mortgage payment on our bungalow house.) That went to charity as well. I also wrote some poems for Allison to distribute to the people in the hospital as encouragements. Mother donated a portion of the money she earned giving piano lessons to March of Dimes. Dad donated carpentry work on the weekends to people in difficult circumstances who needed minor repairs done to their homes.

Allison didn't confine her enthusiasm for volunteer activity just to us. She also started asking neighbors what they could do. If she hadn't been so charming and delightful she would have been very annoying. Most of the neighbors ended up canvassing for March of Dimes. But Allison didn't stop there. She decided one more person ought to be approached about this.

So, she found herself back in her therapist's office on a sunny Thursday afternoon. She had taken the loveseat this time, but since the room had a western exposure, it was rather bright and the sun was shining in her eyes. The counselor kindly got up and pulled the grand drapes shut. They were sheers and let in just enough light to be pleasant.

He sat back down and smiled. "Allison, how are things going?

"Well, I've had a good week at school and an even better week at home," she replied.

"Really? That's encouraging news."

"Yes." She wiped a stray strand of hair out of her eyes. "Well, my volunteering work at the hospital has been fun, but I wanted to see if other people would do something, too."

He smiled. "What have you come up with?"

"I asked my family to do something positive as well. They are all doing different things and are donating their proceeds to charity. The neighbors are helping too."

"That's marvelous!"

"Volunteering and helping other people always make me feel better, and I don't worry about myself quite so much."

He nodded. "That's the idea."

She hesitated just a little. "I was wondering how you would feel about doing something good. Do you volunteer for anything?"

He pushed his glasses up on his nose. "Not at the moment, although I have done so in the past. I think I'd be willing to do some pro bono work for people who need counseling. How would that be?"

"What does 'pro bono' mean?"

"Ah, sorry. It means I would donate my time. Do you think that would be a good service?"

"Oh, yes! Thank you so much. We are all doing this in memory of baby Stevie."

"I'll be happy to."

And that became her last session. She had shaken the counselor's hand and thanked him. Then she took in the wonderful décor, as if memorizing every detail one more time. She had the feeling she would not return. He hadn't suggested another appointment.

At the time, I don't think any of us realized that so much good could come out of so much sadness. But we all volunteered or made donations to help others for years into the future. It was our way of recognizing our tiny miracle worker. Baby Stephen had done it again.

CHAPTER FOURTEEN

THURSDAY

It's Mom's day to be with me. Dad is home as well, and some of the conversation we've been skirting around comes out into the open. It was becoming increasingly apparent that it would benefit Dad if he could do all of his living on the upper floor of the house. In order to make that happen, we'd need to properly cover up the old cellar and build an addition as an extension of the house toward the backyard. He asks Mom if she'll let him sell eighty acres in order to generate cash for the project. She says "no."

I basically kept out of it but continued my cleaning and made a couple of important discoveries. My jeans were looser today, and I found that I was able to get behind the sofa now. Mom agreed, so I seized the opportunity to take down the dust-laden drapes. I took them outside and draped them over an old farm wagon so they could air out. Killer wasn't happy when I went outside. He peered out the screen door, his sweet little cat's head barely visible above the aluminum band at the bottom, and meowed until I went back and picked him up. He scrambled up onto my shoulder because he was afraid of the adult cats. They seemed to wonder what on earth I was doing and why I didn't have cat food.

At one point, I held little Killer out in front of me so I could nuzzle his sweet face. I think he tried to nuzzle me in return because he tried to grab my face. Instead he scratched me; I think it was because he hadn't learned how to keep his tiny claws in yet. Still, it hurt. I went back inside and sat down for a bit of a break, put Killer down, and as punishment, wouldn't let him get in my lap.

Mom decided that I could help her dust her "pretties" that afternoon. All the million little angels were begging to be dusted. I was having trouble getting behind some boxes to reach some of them and at one point almost did the splits. I wondered if the insurance companies knew that dusting could be a hazardous occupation.

I didn't remember millions of angels in our bungalow home. The various collections back then consisted of books and kitchen items, and of course, Dad's war memorabilia, which had made its way downstairs to his workroom. Mother must have started her angel collection after we moved to the farm. Perhaps all of the angels were a way of making her feel better about the house she hated. After all, it was hard to find a spot where angels didn't exist. Or maybe Mother felt that angels were adding consent to her new collections of meaningless items like empty coffee cans, tea bag wrappings, and plastic milk jugs. The milk jugs in particular seemed to be nearly knee-high throughout the kitchen and dining rooms. But whenever I asked Mother about these other items, she always mentioned some potential use she had envisioned for them. It may have been an unspecific use such as "Story Hour" or "Sunday school" but she always held the conviction that these items would be needed someday, and was therefore, extremely reluctant to part with them.

I stayed back where I was, since it had been so much trouble to get there. I dusted everything I could, choosing a knick-knack, dusting it, and then putting it back. I chose a particularly dusty item and looked down at the object in my hand. I was trying to remember the last time I had seen this particular thing. It was right before I had gone to college.

It was an ashtray in the shape of a fire bucket. In fact, it loudly proclaimed "Fire Bucket" on the front in case there was any doubt. I would never give anyone an ashtray today, and I'm not sure why I gave Dad one then. I guess it was because I wanted to show that my gift was especially for him, and smoking was what he did.

It really wasn't a figurine at all, so it was puzzling that it was in among Mom's "pretties" and had been hiding on one of the lower shelves all this time. He'd kept it, even though he had stopped smoking long ago. He'd been to the doctor one day and was told that his blood pressure was so high that he was a walking time bomb. Dad quit cold turkey and had not had a cigarette in twenty years. Yet, he kept the ashtray his little daughter had given him for Christmas one year back in our bungalow house when times were much, much better. Perhaps it was not only a remembrance of the daughter, but also of the way life was for all of us back then. Or maybe it had just been forgotten along with all of the other indistinguishable objects hidden from view.

In spite of his smoking, the bungalow house never smelled like a smoker had lived there. It was nearly always spotless—at least, the main living areas were generally well maintained and usually free of clutter except books. We would never have left had my aunt— Dad's partner in the family farm—not been hospitalized. This aunt was in very bad shape, and Dad foresaw that he would have trouble managing the farm himself from such a distance. Dad's interest in the farm had only been as a business partner, and he had had no interest in running the place. But eventually he convinced Mom that they needed to move, and fortunately for me, they waited until the summer after I had graduated from high school so that I could pursue my study of Latin, which had been my goal to major in during college. I thought it might be a useful major since I had decided I wanted to be an attorney. Surely Latin would be helpful to know as background for all those legal terms. Latin was not offered as a course of study in the new town where my sisters would be attending school.

So the little bungalow house was polished spotlessly clean, listed with a realtor, and sold a week or two before I left to go to college. In fact, when the house was packed up and moved to the farm, I was packed up and moved off to college on the same day.

Grandma sent me a check for $20. She was making good on "Granddaughter Wages." I used it to open a bank account since Mom and Dad had given me no money. They did pay for my room and board, though. Mom wrote me one letter that had a $5 check in it—a pain to take to the bank clear across town—and told me to always keep fresh fruit on hand. It had been after I'd caught a cold, and she wanted me to have some Vitamin C. It was the only spending money they ever sent me during my college days and grad school. Things were just that bad on the farm.

I'd decided I would never work in a restaurant ever again in my life, but I needed spending money, and the only job on campus was for an aide in the natural history museum. Working in the museum would have been okay had it been a desk job. But this position was responsible for tagging dead animals, and I just could not bring myself to apply for that one. There was a position at a local doughnut shop, but I jettisoned that idea as well. I'd had enough Cock-a-Doodle Doughnuts to last a lifetime. I ended up working as a waitress for a steakhouse and earned real wages this time, too.

The first Christmas at the new little house on the farm was the worst ever. Mother didn't even bother to put up any decorations. Maybe she couldn't find them; I could perhaps forgive her for that. There were boxes and more boxes strewn around the living area in addition to completely taking up the basement. But the gifts were disgusting. I received a remnant of fabric. That was it. Dad recounted days from the Depression and how he might receive a pencil or tablet for school. That would be it—nothing else. I suppose that helped put it in perspective. I made myself a vest and skirt and got myself off our little farm and back to school as quickly as I could. I understood how Mom felt. She hated the new house that had no character, and so did I. They had not made a place for me. There was no space for me to call my own; I had not felt welcome there. I hated the boxes stacked throughout and the lack of Christmas decorations. This would never be my home.

Grandma was good about writing once I got back to college. Mother's letters, on the other hand, were extremely sporadic and empty of anything newsworthy except reminders that Jesus was my very best friend. Grandma's letters were lively and newsy, and although she was barely scraping by, there was usually always a few dollars or even a five- or ten-dollar bill in every letter I opened. When there was no money in the envelope, there would at least be a few postage stamps or a stick of gum, usually Wrigley's Juicy Fruit or Doublemint Gum. Sometimes Grandma sent a stick of Wrigley's Spearmint Gum, but you could be sure that she would never send any Sour Stink Gum.

I'd asked her once how I could ever repay her. I was certain that she'd sent me far more than I had actually earned in "Granddaughter Wages." Although she did not call it that, she introduced me to the concept of "paying it forward." She said, "You'll help your little cousins when they go to college. And when you have children of your own, you'll help them."

That first year in college was very tough. It was harder to keep in touch then. Long-distance calls were expensive. Letters took too long to arrive. Mom and Dad were dealing with the difficulties of an unfinished house and other troublesome matters. Money was always tight, and then I came home to all of the shock of unfinished bathrooms and disarray and the pickle, biscuit, and tea diet. I think that was really when Mom's OCD began in earnest. There may have been hints of it before like after little Stevie had died. She was always a bit of a packrat. But she had always been able to throw things out before, and she'd always been able to recognize trash for what it was: trash.

I think the clutter of all the belongings still in boxes with no proper place to call home paved the way for clutter to become comfortable. She could control that because it could not move unless it was at her direction. Dad was to leave the stuff alone. It was her way of punishing him for making her move to a house she didn't love. Although they'd jointly chosen the floor plan, she would never be happy there because it wasn't built "old" with character. It was a cookie-cutter house from a cookie-cutter company. Mom's mind was made up. She would not be happy in that house and would make sure to hate it every day of her life. And not only that, but she would also make sure Dad knew that she hated it every day of *his* life as well.

Once, after a rain, I heard her yelling in the basement, "I hate you, I hate you, I hate you!" I wondered whom on earth she was screaming at. I went downstairs and saw that there was water throughout the basement, and Mom was in the southwest corner in ankle-deep water, facing the tiny window and screaming at the wall. That was where the leaking had come from, and it had thrown her over the edge.

I was pulled out of my reverie when a voice said, "Kelly, would you like a cup of tea?" Mom was on the other side of the room and had just put down her dust cloth. I put mine down on one of the bookshelves I had been dusting, carefully maneuvered my way out of the corner, and sat down on an edge of the sofa that hadn't been entirely cleared yet. Dad was asleep in his recliner, his little bird chest heaving in and out.

I still needed to look for my jewelry box, but I could save that for tomorrow. We still needed to go get the drapes that had been airing outside all day long and bring them back inside. That was going to be enough of a project for one day.

CHAPTER FIFTEEN
THURSDAY—PART TWO

Mother had gone into town to run an errand after we had put the drapes back up, and I got a sudden burst of energy again. I decided to try to tackle the dining room. I remembered we had an old stereo cabinet in one of the corners. Maybe I could take some of my old LPs back home with me. (For my younger readers, vinyl LPs, also called albums, were the precursors to CDs. They were revolutionary because before then, every song was recorded as a single. Several songs were on an LP, short for "Long Playing.")

I identified the corner in which the stereo cabinet had last stood and began attempting to make my way over there with a big trash bag and a dust cloth. I kicked more empty plastic milk jugs out of the way. There were boxes and many things piled around the dining room table, as high as the table. As I was making my way toward the corner, which was taking quite some time given all of the stuff I was trying to maneuver around, I came upon a photo of my mother's family when they were children. Grandma and Grandpa were looking very happy, and Mother's brother and sister were looking very happy as well. Mother was smiling, but there was something about her eyes that seemed a little off. There was something behind them that she was unable to mask in front of the camera. Maybe it was just me, but it seemed like she was hiding a distasteful secret. I guessed her to be about ten or eleven years old. I dusted the framed photograph and put it back on top of the swelling dining room table. There was no place else to put it.

I finally made my way back to the corner after straddling a couple of big piles. There it was! The old console was covered with piles of cloths (maybe unused tea towels), old figurines, more dried flower arrangements, and a cookie jar.

Hey! I remembered that cookie jar. It was in a style popular in the late fifties, and we had had that ever since our Stephen house. I dusted off the lid and the sides, and then I picked it up. Surely not! Something was rattling around inside it. I set it back down and removed the lid. Sure enough, Snickerdoodle cookies from God knew how long ago. Petrified. I'd hazard a guess that they'd been there since I had come home for Christmas my freshman year in college more than thirty years ago. I was the only person who ever baked cookies. I loved chocolate chip cookies, but Mother never bought the chips because they were too expensive. But Snickerdoodles were easy, and we usually had the ingredients on-hand because they were basics and tended to be used for other cooking.

But now that I thought about it, Mother had actually baked cookies once. That was a remarkable day because she was just not the cookie-baking type. She would bake pies, and once in a great while, a cake, but for her to bake cookies, now that was really something.

It was the day I had turned eleven years old. She'd risen early, and in between taking care of Allison, who was having an asthma attack, and seeing to Reese, who had awakened with the flu, Mom had baked cookies for me to take to school. They were sugar cookies, cut with a Santa Claus cutter. It was the only proper cookie cutter we had. I admit I was a little disappointed at the shape (this was January), but I knew better than to complain. I secretly did wish she had taken a cup or glass, or even a clean, empty tin can, and turned it upside-down to use as a cutter, but at least I was going to have treats to take to school that year. The cookie cutter had been a gift from Santa Claus the previous Christmas. Evidently he had known that I was taking cooking in 4-H. I'd baked some refrigerator cookies the previous summer, and they had won a blue ribbon at the County Fair!

I counted the cookies very carefully, examining each one to make sure they were perfect. As I counted, I wondered why Mother always had to ruin things for me. Even when she was attempting to do a nice thing for me, she always seemed to do it not quite all the way, or to make it a little off, like baking Santa Claus cookies in January. When she did things like that, it seemed like she was telling me that I wasn't worthy or that I wasn't deserving of her efforts. Why did she hate me so much?

I finally finished my checking and counting. There were twenty-two cookies. There were twenty-one kids in my class including me, and I needed one for Warren Gustafson, who lived a block away. Warren would come over to our house, and we would walk to school together. Warren wasn't in my class that year; that's why I needed the extra cookie. Warren had just arrived, and I thanked Mom for the cookies; then Warren and I left the house. Once we got down the block a little bit (so Mom wouldn't see, in case she was watching), I let him pick one. The snow was swirling around us, and Warren's red scarf and hat made a nice contrast to the white snow. I could see some of his sandy, wavy hair stubbornly peeking out from under the brim of his hat. Warren reached in the bag carefully and pulled the cookie on top out quickly so the snow wouldn't drift in on the others. He gave me a quizzical look when he noticed the shape, but then said, "Hmm! This looks good!" I had been concerned about his reaction, but needn't have been. Warren was always very kind. He broke off the part of the cookie that was the Santa's pack and gave it to me. "Happy birthday, Kelly!"

I blushed and said, "Thank you." He smiled. And walking in the snow with Warren and having something to share with him was the happiest thing ever.

It was a lucky thing that Reese was sick that day. I know that if she'd been with us, I would not have had any cookies left by the time I got to school. I still hadn't been able to forgive her for eating all my Easter candy when I was in the second grade. And how on earth she ever grew up to be skinnier than me was more than I'd ever be able to understand.

But that day it was just Warren and me, the swirling snow, and my Santa Claus cookies. And they were good. It was the happiest day of my life.

Well, it was happy until that afternoon when it was time for treats. I could hear the whispering in the background:

"Her mother made treats this year!"

"Yeah, but they are cookies shaped like Santa Claus." There was much snickering.

"Well, at least she has treats this year. They're poor you know, those Jones people."

"Yeah, her brother had a big head."

Luckily, Mrs. Boylan, my fifth grade teacher, not only had eyes in the back of her head, but also had supersonic ears. She rose to my defense. "Well, isn't this interesting! Sugar cookies shaped like Santa Claus! How marvelous that we can have a reminder of our wonderful Christmas vacation! And aren't we fortunate to have Kelly in our class! Did you know that today is Kansas Day? Yes! Kansas was admitted to the Union on January 29, 1861! She must be a *real* Kansas girl!"

The snickering stopped, and now there were hums of admiration. God bless Mrs. Boylan. (I didn't see the need to mention that Colorado was the state of my birth.) After we ate my treats, I got to choose the game I wanted to play that day: State Capitols or Spelling Bee. I chose State Capitols. Warren wasn't in the class for me to impress with my spelling prowess anyway. But I knew I would have won. Excellence had become important to me.

And the day improved that evening with Grandma's visit and gifts. The first one was my very first watch, a Timex. And the second was the lovely cream jewelry box with the ballerina that I now so desperately wanted to find.

Ah, Warren. I'd been in love with that man since we were both six years old. Our families were friends; his father had worked with my grandfather when Grandpa was still alive. My earliest memory of him was at his house. Warren was alternating jumping on the furniture, trying to see how high he could go without falling, or holding his breath, reddening his face to nearly purple before he finally had to give up and fill his lungs again. He was definitely trying to win my heart, and it worked.

Dang, he was handsome. Wavy, light-brown hair and green eyes. He had that Patrick Swayze look. And yes, he did come into the Shiloh Café and Grill for coffee on that day with his parents when they were moving back from the East Coast.

It was a fine summer day in the late 1960s. Marie, Roger, and Warren walked into the place, and I found I literally could not breathe. Warren was wearing a tie-dyed hunter green tank top. It brought out his green eyes. He'd either been doing manual labor or working out at a gym and was tanned. Warren Gustafson was a Scandinavian god. Grandma sat at a booth with them and kept a running commentary going. I was seated at a table across from them along with Allison and Reese, who were doing silly things. I could feel time slipping through my fingers. Warren was being polite and was listening to Grandma's update. Perhaps out of shyness for both of us, neither of us approached the other but simply said hello and good-bye.

When they left, Grandma said, "Next time, Kelly, you need to grab Warren by the arm and tell him you'll show him around town!" Dang it, Grandma, why didn't you suggest that when they were here? Showing him around wouldn't have occurred to me; after all, they had lived in this very town.

The next time I saw him was a few years after they'd visited the restaurant. We were both graduating from high school. It was 1972. They'd moved back to the Midwest, but lived about five or six hours from us. We were visiting relatives in the area, and Marie had invited us to stop by.

Warren was still as handsome as ever. I wished I'd had a picture of him. I asked about his plans after high school. He said he was joining the military. Oh, God. Vietnam. Did he still play the trumpet? No, he played the guitar now. We played Parcheesi for a while. Then I took Grandma's advice this time and touched him lightly on the arm when we had finished a round. I asked if he felt like going outside. We went for a walk down a little tree-covered lane, sparked with forest ferns here and there. The canopy was yellowed with flickering sunlit patches like the design of a dappled horse's coat. We were holding hands; it felt like we had never been apart. Suddenly the awning of trees became the swirling snow, and it was as though we were walking to school, sharing Santa Claus cookies. Warren leaned over and kissed me lightly on the cheek. It was brief but sufficient: it curled my toes and set my heart beating to music that only love could understand. Suddenly, Marie was calling us for dinner; just as we emerged from the lane, Warren asked for my address so we could keep in touch. We dropped hands as we entered the yard. I didn't need Allison and Reese going at it again. They would probably tease me anyway, without any additional kindling.

Warren entered basic training then Vietnam. Our letters sailed across the seas as if beckoned by an unassailable force, each one with greater conviction and urgency. I treasured every single scrap and would run my hand over the paper where his hand had been as he wrote. One of the more significant letters contained a photo of my soldier boy perched atop a tank, helmet on but chin strap loose. In that letter he asked me to wait for him. I couldn't write back fast enough—of course I would wait! We began making plans long-distance. They were just vague ideas since we didn't know exactly when he would come home. But plans were definitely being laid. First we would shop for my ring, and then we would look at wedding reception venues. The church was easy. I decided I could start looking at dresses and flowers at any time.

During one of the breaks in college while I was back on the farm, a letter arrived from Marie. Mother showed it to me, and I took it outside to read. It was a warm, humid summer morning: the air was heavy. I can even now feel the way the earth sighed beneath my feet as I read the news, but I had already known; somewhere within myself I had felt something escape. The best part of me had left. It was not coming back. And now the kindness that had been Warren became the dew on the grass, lending sweet moisture to the soft earth. And the spark that had been Warren was now the mischievous breeze playing with my hair. Warren was everywhere yet nowhere. Two birds suddenly emerged from the old buckeye tree and took flight in tandem toward the heavens.

I came to my senses and dumped the petrified Snickerdoodles into the trash bag along with several stray tears. I wiped my eye on my shirtsleeve. Then I decided to try to open the stereo cabinet but found that I would need to clear a bigger pathway between it and the dining room table before I would be able to open the doors. I was suddenly feeling very weary and decided to abandon that idea for today. I would just end up finding more upsetting memories inside the cabinet once I got it open, anyway. Like the album Warren had given me for Christmas. A remnant of Joni Mitchell's song, "Both Sides Now" suddenly came rushing into my head, and I knew it would be with me the rest of the day:

> It's love's illusions I recall
> I really don't know love at all
>
> —Joni Mitchell

I began making my way back around the dining room table to Mother's chair where Killer leapt into my arms. He seemed to know I needed his help.

CHAPTER SIXTEEN

FRIDAY

It's Friday, and Mom has gone to work today; Dad and I are ready to do some new things. I was exhausted when I arrived at the house, and Dad invited me to sit down while he worked the Jumble in the newspaper. He could work that thing like nobody's business. He wanted to take a little nap after that, so he slept in his chair, and I dozed until my bug bites itched too much for me to ignore. Besides, he was starting to snore.

I did a little more work around the living room while he slept. I was satisfied with progress in there, but looking at all of the empty plastic milk jugs strewn all over the kitchen floor was driving me crazy. I started clearing all that mess out. There were coffee cans all over the place, too. They all had stuff in them. I opened one and discovered that it was nearly full to the brim of lids from the plastic milk jugs. Why was she saving all of this stuff?

Her old antique mason jars above the cabinets were begging to be dusted, but it seemed just too overwhelming even to think about doing that. They were nearly all black around the necks of the jars where the dust was just that thick. Looking down toward the bottom of each jar revealed its true color: either clear or a teal color, popular in the early 1900s. I could see why it might be difficult to get motivated to clean anything when everything you touched would turn into another project.

Dad woke up after about an hour and decided to run into town to do some grocery shopping. He gathered up his oxygen apparatus, and I helped him go down the stairs and out to the car. It was a warm day, and the cats were sunning themselves again. A head or two peered up lazily when they heard Dad going to the car.

I stayed behind to do more work in the entry and kitchen. I'd also decided to try to find my jewelry box. I made my way down the now relatively passable hall and looked in Mom and Dad's bedroom. It was the bedroom that had once been designated as mine. I thought my jewelry box would still be on the chest of drawers where I had left it, but stuff was packed from floor to ceiling, and I could not see past it at all. Your choices, as you entered the room, were either to take a few steps forward and hop on the bed, or to turn around and go back out the room. There was literally that little space to move about in—maybe an area of three-feet-by-two-feet—smaller than Dad's tiny spot. The part of the room at the foot of the bed was somewhat visible although blocked by a large Styrofoam box of some sort. It was at least six-feet-by-three-feet. It was too wide for me to scale over, and the wall of stuff to the side of the bed prevented seeing anything beyond, even from the foot of the bed. I gave up and decided I didn't really need my jewelry box that badly.

Suddenly I heard Dad down in the entry. "Kelly, can you help me?" he pled with urgency. I leapt off the bed and hurried out of the room and back down the hall.

I could see him at the bottom of the stairs with two heavy plastic bags of groceries cutting into his hands. I ran down and pried the plastic from around his fingers. The bags were so heavy, and he had taken so long to hobble to the house from the car, that the weight had dug red marks into his hands. One of the bags contained a frozen blueberry pie. "We'll just let that set out, Kelly, and have a little snack later on." Since the pie was already baked, we'd be able to eat it once it thawed. I'd never had cool blueberry pie before, but it tasted great that hot afternoon.

The entry began to look better as I arranged the baby eucalyptus I'd purchased earlier that week in some old antique crocks. It made the place smell marvelous. I'd also purchased some yellow mums in town and put those in the front yard to help define the entrance. I couldn't stand the place looking so trashy, with an ill-defined entrance. Dad coughed behind me as we came up the stairs. "Do you think I could use one of your new storage bins to keep my winter clothes in?"

"Of course, Dad!" We went outside and put one in the backseat of his car. I'd brought his clean clothes back from Reese's for him, and we put them in the bin for him. "At least I'll know where my winter clothes are," he remarked rather hopefully, I thought. This was August. He was worrying about his winter clothes in *August.*

I spent the rest of the afternoon cleaning more of the entry, living room, and kitchen and hauling out the trash. I counted sixty-four bags for that week. I put them temporarily on one side of Dad's car—the side furthest from the road—in case Mom came home early. I didn't want her to see the filled trash bags as she drove up; otherwise she might want to go through the trash to see what we were throwing out. We'd been hauling the trash over to Allen and Reese's every night so Mom wouldn't see the bags leaving the house.

When I came back inside, Dad asked me to throw out the pickle juice that Mom had been saving. There were about eight jars sitting around the kitchen counters. Then he wanted me to throw out all of the bacon grease Mom had been saving. I thought I could dump that in one of the bags that wasn't quite full. When I went outside, it was as if I had adopted the persona of the Pied Piper. Every cat in the farmyard immediately roused and followed me all the way out to the garbage bags. Evidently Mom had been truthful when she'd said that she mixed in the old bacon grease with the cat food.

I looked around while I was trying to dump the old grease in one of the bags and noticed the old rabbit hutch was still out back. Reese had kept rabbits when she was in high school, and the hutch was still there.

I went back inside and did a little more work. I am not sure what possessed me, but I took the old hassock, which was beyond its useful life, and put it in a black, plastic trash bag. I hauled it out to the old hen house, which was also beyond its useful life, and threw the bag as hard as I could into the hen house, where the old hassock could die a peaceful death. At least there would be a little more space in the living room now.

The downside would be that I'd have to lie to Mom when she wanted to know where her hassock was.

I thought better of it that evening and asked Lars to retrieve it if I didn't remember to do that before I left. I'd pay to have it reupholstered for her.

CHAPTER SEVENTEEN

SATURDAY

We stood on the ridge on which the house was built, enjoying the pretty scenery from that vantage point. There were many prairie flowers sprinkled like tiny polka dots among the grasses in the pastures. The warm greens of the background with the tiny bright colors interspersed made the scene reminiscent of voile or lawn Dotted Swiss fabric. I never tired of the beauty of the Kansas landscape, or the panoramic horizon.

Mom invited me to walk down the hill with her, toward the rabbit hutch, and we picked our way along the muddy path. She wanted to show me where she planned to plant her annual pumpkin patch. Of course, she never took her own car for sales expeditions once the pumpkins had ripened; she relied on Reese, Allen, and their pick-up truck. The compost heap was at least fifty yards away, so the fruits of her labors there would have to be transported over to the garden. She kept an old wheelbarrow under the rabbit hutch, which was near the future site of her intended pumpkin patch. We had left the wheelbarrow alone when we were cleaning up the yard. I didn't bring up the subject of the location of the compost heap; I figured that was a closed chapter.

We'd had rain the night before, but now the skies to the east were clear and bright. To the southwest, rain clouds were forming. The clear skies might be short-lived. The prairie wind was blowing lightly, but it was the warm wind of August. The trees stirred in the breeze; here and there, a tree might be in the way of the expansive view, but in nearly every direction I could clearly see where the soft, warm, green fabric met distant blue.

I picked up a long leaf of grass and started chewing on it. I looked behind me where all of the trash bags had been piled not twelve hours before. Luckily, the rain had washed away all telltale signs, and I was willing to bet that Mother would not notice all of the stuff that we had thrown out. I didn't think she could possibly have made emotional attachments to all of the articles I had disposed of, like the endless supply of empty plastic milk jugs. There was still plenty more where that came from.

She bent down and picked a stray weed from the path, her long caftan billowing out behind her. I pondered this. She could tell that the weed didn't belong there, but couldn't see the trash within her own home that should be cast aside just like that weed. I kept going back to what we'd learned about OCD and hoarding from the helpful internet sites and wondered what bad thing she thought would happen if she threw stuff out. Would she never get counseling? She had, after all, seen its benefits both in her own daughter and mother.

We reached the rabbit hutch, and Mother started recounting a story. Mother would often tell me little vignettes about her story hour or Sunday school kids and the funny and cute things they would say and do. It had been her version of therapy to the extent that it seemed that as long as Mom had small children in her life—presumably to make up for her own lost children—she'd be happy, or relatively so, the house notwithstanding.

There was a little girl whose grandpa owned a general store out on Highway 12 not too far out of a little town in over in Oshonee County. She loved rabbits, and he'd agreed that she could keep some in a little hutch in back of the store. She lived just down the block with her mom, dad, and younger siblings, but her parents didn't want a hutch in their yard, so the grandpa had said that she could keep her bunnies over behind the general store. Besides, it wouldn't be so far to carry the heavy sacks of rabbit food from the store if the rabbits were kept in back.

She had three bunnies, all girls. There was a brown and white one with a white tail (Hoppy), a black and white one (Blackie), and a pretty, little gray one (Flossie). One warm spring day, she was out in the back feeding the rabbits in the hutch. She heard a sudden commotion and saw to her bewilderment some men with guns who were frog-marching her grandfather out the rear door of the building. She ducked down and hid behind a bush near the hutch but could still see what was going on. He was begging them to take the money and just leave. But they weren't going to let him off that easy. They stripped him naked, started beating him, gagged him, and then tied him to a tree. During a lull in their conversation when they were debating about whether to kill him, she sneezed.

"Hank, did you hear that?"

"Idiot, why are you calling me by my name? The old man will remember that, Clem. Now we'll have to kill him for sure."

"Who are you calling an idiot? You just did it yourself. "

"Did what?"

"Called me by my name! Now, shut up and listen! I thought I heard something sneeze. Over here."

They started walking in the direction of the sneeze, carefully walking around the grounds, and finally spotted a bit of her pink dress poking out behind the bush. The dress would have been ideal in an overgrown summer garden but was entirely wrong for hiding behind the bush that hadn't fully leafed out yet.

They pulled her into the open.

"Hey, I think she could use some good lovin'!"

"Hey, I think so, too!"

They dragged her to the shed behind the store where all of the cleaning supplies were housed. She kicked and screamed, but it was no use. They took the grandfather's clothes with them into the smelly shed. Then something happened in the dark shed that hurt. She didn't understand it. The men threatened to kill both her and her grandfather if she told anybody about it. They had gagged her with her panties but uncovered her mouth just long enough for her to say that she wouldn't tell. Then they gagged her again and left her in the dark shed with the overpowering odors of the cleaning supplies. They pinned the shed tight-closed with the big peg across the door outside.

About a half hour later, a customer stumbled into quite a mess inside the store. He called and called inside the store; he knew the proprietor well, and this was just not right. He called some more, and then decided to walk around outside. He discovered the grandpa, tied to the tree in back. The old gentleman had been gagged but not blindfolded. After freeing the old man and giving him his jacket to cover up with, the Good Samaritan was about to go call the police. But the grandpa was mutely pointing to the shed; he was unable to speak. Tears were flooding his cheeks. The customer ran over to the shed where he discovered the girl. She was lying on her side in a fetal position, rocking and sobbing. The old man finally stood up and tied the jacket around his waist, then hobbled over to the shed, and gathered his sweet, little granddaughter in his arms. The customer called the police from the pay phone just outside the entrance to the store, and they arrived with an ambulance in tow.

The girl was taken to the hospital but kicked and fought so hard that the medical team could not do a proper examination. She was sedated and kept overnight.

I could stand it no more. "Why are you telling me this horrible story?" I demanded.

Mother stopped talking and gave me a pointed look with those blue eyes. Just then, a huge clap of thunder exploded, and I could see some lightning streaking across the sky to the southwest out of the corner of my eye. The storm was coming.

"Because you needed to know," she said, gently.

I gazed into those same blue eyes those predators had peered into, and I retched until only bile came up.

Mother rubbed my back while my sick spilled over the damp earth. When I was finally able to raise my head, she said, "I was ten years old."

I retched some more.

"It all started with rabbits. It was a long time before I could agree to let Reese keep them." And she turned and started toward the house.

The sky had grown dark and now big pellets of rain were beginning to shoot to the ground like hammers. I retched one last time, and my sick ran down little gullies with the sudden downpour. Everything was going toward the proposed site of the pumpkin patch. I let the rain wash over me as if it could absolve me of the horrible secret.

When I had finally finished, the whole enormity of it all hit me as if my face had been slapped. It wasn't enough that Mom had lost two sons and had experienced a difficult move; she had had a childhood trauma that had taken everything from her, and now through the process of unbidden accumulation, was trying to preserve everything that she had.

God! Had the hoarding trigger occurred in adolescence? I remembered Grandma had mentioned once that Mother had started her book collection around the time she was ten or eleven years old. She escaped into a different world through her books; the real world had been too unpleasant. Suddenly, everything fit: the aversion to cleaning products; the inability to stand up for herself or others; the sense of loss; the frequent escapes into other worlds that only books or gardening contained; the rapid development of a backbone when there was a threat to physical or personal safety in a young one; the abrupt personality change in the face of an unexpected, severe, and inconveniencing event, like burying a dog or seeing to pee sheets. She had lost more than anybody I had ever known, and the signs had been in front of me all along. Lord, I was slower than a Lilliputian scaling Mount Everest: the unfolding disgusting truth was even more than I had been able to imagine.

CHAPTER EIGHTEEN
SATURDAY—PART TWO

We spent the rest of the day sorting through Sunday school materials. Occasionally Mother would point out some special lesson and what some faceless child had learned from her. She'd touched a number of lives. She spoke fondly of her own Sunday schoolteachers. I wondered if life might have turned out differently for her if she'd been able to tell one of them her terrible secret.

I didn't say much. I figured if she wanted to talk more about it, she'd bring it up. But I was hoping she would avoid the topic. I was shocked that Grandma hadn't reported on this, but it was so heinous, there must be some things that even Grandma could filter out and keep to herself. Yet all this time, Mother had never spoken of it. She had somehow been able to avoid becoming an abuser herself. We were yelled at and sometimes struck, made to march around the house in pee sheets, but never molested. She never touched any child inappropriately.

Mother talked a bit more about her Sunday schoolteachers, who certainly deserved a lot of the credit. Jesus was truly her salvation; church was safe. She would often stay after church and help with cleaning up the hospitality table. Church her second family, a family who validated her and with whom she felt secure. She did all of the extra activities, and Jesus became her very best friend. She was able to understand the kind of love that Jesus gave.

Eventually she'd been able to forgive those men. But it took a long time of going to Sunday school and praying. She would pray silently at church on Sunday and ask God for forgiveness. Like a true victim, she blamed herself and wondered if she had encouraged the transgression. But she was never able to verbalize anything about the incident to anyone. It might have helped if she could have at least told a teacher. Of course, the grandpa knew, and so did her parents, but this sort of thing was hushed up back then.

The predators had taken her spirit and her sense of self-esteem. She became powerless. Before the incident, if there had been trouble on the playground, she would normally have taken care of it. She'd been a natural leader, popular and a good student. Her studies didn't suffer after the attack; in fact, she threw herself into her books even more aggressively than before. But the shift in her interactions with others took a massive step backward, and other children began to recognize that they could take advantage of her goodness. She never fought back and never felt worthy of anything, no matter how small.

Lord, I had no clue. All these years I spent hating my mother for the way she was, and now my hatred was levied at those two horrible men. I wondered if they'd been abused as boys. We'd never know, but I did know this: I hoped with all my heart that they were rotting in hell with Hitler and the rest.

And now I was going to have to work on this forgiveness thing and try to forgive myself for all of the awful things I had thought about her all those years, and for all of the ill will I had harbored. I still had not been able to forgive Reese for eating all of my Easter candy when I was about seven years old. How was I going to forgive myself for something much worse that had gone on for much longer? Further, I had to forgive Mom for all of the things she'd done to me whether out of spite or just because she couldn't help the way she was.

We stopped for a break and went upstairs. I sat in the chair with Killer while Mom went in to brew some tea. Dad had just awakened from his nap.

They continued their conversation regarding a possible upstairs expansion to the house. Dad was going to go check with the bank on Monday since they'd decided not to sell any land. And I wrapped up the week knowing that I'd done the best I could. The house looked a little better, but it would certainly be a losing battle unless Mom got counseling.

I heard from Mom and Dad the following week. The bank had approved their loan, and a new addition would be built to extend the house on the upper level to the east. Hopefully this would give Mom some more room, but I worried that it would all become as cluttered as the rest of the house. A local contractor would be hired at a discount since Mom and Dad were close personal friends.

I got photos at Christmas. It did look grand. They'd bought a pot-bellied stove that looked rather out of place in the cookie-cutter house, but if they were happy, I was happy. The old cellar had been covered entirely, and an enclosed closet now safely disguised the entrance to the basement in that part of the house. The same contractor had built some beautiful units in which to display china and provide a large buffet space. It finally was becoming the home we'd all hoped it would be. But best of all, Dad wouldn't be living in an area the size of a dog cage anymore.

So it was especially disappointing when I walked in about two years later to find that nothing had changed, really. The new addition was now full of boxes and new detritus that Mother couldn't part with. The grand windows were partly blocked by stuff piled up to eye level. It would have been a marvelous view otherwise. The dark paneling made a sinister backdrop for all of the mounds and piles. The new laundry room— intended to make their lives easier—had taken on the personality of storage closet. Dad was not bathing upstairs, and he could not take a nap on the couch. And worst of all, he had gone back to his tiny area, which looked even smaller now with the grand expanse of the new addition, which had become Mom's space.

The house stank as badly as it had before, Killer had become a rangy, anti-social outdoor cat, and I couldn't wait to leave the place behind again.

I learned later that the six rugs we had so painstakingly moved to the decrepit white Lincoln had been returned to the bathtub "where they belong."

CHAPTER NINETEEN
MANY EXCITING DISCOVERIES

It was much easier the second time around. Mother actually cooperated. Of course, we'd gone about it entirely wrong the first time, just forging ahead like ravenous, uncontrollable dogs in pursuit of a fox, cleaning and pitching whatever we wanted.

She described it later as "surreal." I don't think she was thinking about all the years associated with the accumulation of what were now discards, but rather the actual reconciliation of all the memories that she'd connected to the lost belongings, and a letting go of what had caused it all. It was as if the inferno had the power to cleanse battered remembrances.

This time, the entire mission was different, and Mother stood in front of the bonfire in the role of a caesarean master judge, nodding the fate of every article that had been stacked floor-to-ceiling in the basement. Thumbs up, thumbs down. Some things were to be thrown in the fire, others to be salvaged for some noble purpose. Usually it was not a matter of deciding anything but simply getting the ruined item out of sight quickly in order to be rid of the disgusting mold or other filth that now consumed it. Of course, along with the destruction of the item also went the emotional attachment that had been so important for the thirty previous years and which had continued to summon

Mother to the basement whenever it rained so that all of the important memories could be moved, stacked somewhere else, compartmentalized, and salvaged.

One of the odd things she'd decided to keep was a felt-covered, heart-shaped box that must have been a long-ago home to some Valentine's Day candy. "What are you going to use that for, Mom?" Reese wanted to know.

"I'll probably use it for Story Hour sometime," Mom replied. True to herself, Mother always had something in mind, some dream for everything she saved.

Story Hour had featured prominently in Mom's life after they moved to the farm. She enjoyed being around "little people," especially after her own children and grandchildren had matured. Most of us had experienced the feeling of being set aside in favor of her "little people." It had happened to me in college when the first granddaughter had been born. No love or attention was ever lost on that little girl, and I'd loved my little first niece, too. But I didn't feel I was getting the attention I needed from Mom and Dad. I noticed that no expense was ever spared with that child, whereas my own needs seemed to be ignored. I'm sure it wasn't really intentional on their part; the pattern of having little people in Mom's life had long been established through her Story Hour ministry to the local kids. She won awards and was written up in newspapers. It gave her the encouragement and recognition she'd never had before.

She steadied herself again as the next object, an old sofa from the 1960s, was presented for her to determine its fate. Really, there was no question. The old sofa had to go. But protocol was observed, and Mom nodded toward the fire. As if it had been clapped by lightning, the sofa immediately burst into flames, shooting sparks everywhere and causing the observers to jump backward a few feet to relative safety. Flames lapped at the object as if in evil delight. The old sofa would have been a certain fire hazard had the basement not already been a fairly damp place. The leaky pipe just got the ball rolling.

Dad had received an $800 water bill, quite a princely sum for a little two-story house. A leak, powerful enough to cause water damage up to four or five feet from the basement floor, was the culprit. The basement, barely passable except through a few paths in the floor-to-ceiling debris, had had to be entirely emptied and cleaned, and the lower four-to-five-feet stripped of its sheetrock. Fortunately, everything above the water level was salvaged. But the basement had always been a relatively damp place, and the mold must have been present even before then. That must have been the horrible odor throughout the house: mold.

The great basement excavation revealed many astonishing discoveries. One of the most memorable was the disgusting shock of seeing what lay underneath the old sofa when it was carried out. At first glance, the seventies shag carpeting had changed color from pale lime green to oyster white. But wait—did it get puffier? And why did it seem to be waving in places? The carpet flooring had become so damp that mushrooms had taken root, their ugly white heads appearing to nod at passers-by, or gawkers as the case may be. Dad was outside when another shocker, the old mattress from the bed they'd slept on all those pre-obsessive-compulsive disorder years was carried out. The fabric seemed to be very dark and in perpetual motion, as if it were wiggling. Upon closer inspection, one could see that it was covered entirely with bugs. "Lots of good memories there," Dad quipped. Every one of us had been conceived on that mattress, except Miss Back-Seat-of-the-Car: me. The unwanted child.

Lars uncovered a number of mouse skeletons, and they'd died, according to him, in vain attempts to be rid of their unbelievably horrible living conditions. There was a pile of fur in one of the closets, and Allen was afraid some groundhog or other creature had died there. Turns out, all the fur had fallen off a coat I'd had in high school, my "huggy bear" coat. The shell of the coat itself was still on the hanger, the fur long since separated from the fabric and presently adorning the closet floor.

There were stacks and stacks of canned foods from "when Moses was a baby" all grouped together in rotting cardboard boxes. The meat in the old deep freeze was long since gone. The mangle ironer was in mint condition, and glory be, the Stradivarius violin recovered! It had been preserved with thirty-five years of neglect. They found little Jason's clothes. Mother could hang on to those and vicariously touch the little baby that death had stolen so quickly. I thought it was sort of like a Bible being discovered completely intact after a fire, flood, or some other disaster.

Along with the canned foods was a half case of bottled salad dressing. Upon closer inspection, the bottles read, "Labeled for Restaurant Use Only. Not for Retail Sale." They were bottles of Seven Seas Italian Dressing. I smiled at the memory.

Little Maria Dover had been asking Grandma please to offer Italian dressing. Grandma had three choices of dressings: Blue Cheese, Thousand Island, and French, made available to customers in attractive silver tri-pod servers. (The French dressing was a bright orange concoction that was so sweet it made me feel as though I had the power to whistle "Dixie" straight out my ears.) If someone ordered a salad, we took one of the tri-pod servers over to them. Grandma had told Maria that she didn't think Italian dressing would sell well in the café.

"This is an American restaurant. People want American salad dressings. I don't think 'Eye-talian' will sell well."

"Yes, ma'am, but you are already serving French dressing." Grandma didn't have a good retort for this, although as I found out later when I studied in France, the American sweet, orange-colored version of French salad dressing of the 1960s was not the same as real French salad dressing served in France, which is basically an oil and vinegar infusion, or vinaigrette. But Grandma didn't know that, and neither did I. She was in fact, serving American dressing labeled French. But absent this knowledge, Maria had a pretty strong point.

Grandma was a compassionate employer in addition to being a very good businesswoman. She had had a very good morning, and was in a good mood. She had just finished teaching me how to price a special, and she had taught Reese how to count back change.

"Now, Reese, a customer has come in and ordered three specials and a child's plate with a hot chocolate. Their coffee is included in the specials, so that makes the total seven dollars and ninety-three cents. The customer gives you a twenty-dollar bill. Now count the change back for me."

Reese began, "Seven ninety-three, ninety-four, ninety-five, and eight dollars," she said, handing Grandma two pennies and then a nickel. She continued, "Now that's eight dollars, nine, ten," handing Grandma two dollars. She concluded "ten and twenty" handing Grandma a ten-dollar bill.

"Now how much change have you given the customer?"

Reese replied, "Twelve dollars and seven cents."

"Eeeee! That's exactly right!" Grandma exclaimed, then told Reese she was looking down her shirt front to make sure all of her buttons were still there, she was so proud.

Grandma wiped her hands on her apron and thought for a little bit about Maria's point. She told Maria that if she could get fifty people to sign a petition saying they wanted Shiloh Café and Grill to serve Italian dressing, she would do so. Grandma was no fool; this was free advertising.

Little Maria had gone up and down Petunia Street and up and down Main Street to all of the merchants. She also begged Reggie to ask customers in their little convenience store to sign the petition.

Sure enough, Maria got her fifty signatures. Grandma stood by her word, and began serving "Eye-talian" dressing. But given that she wasn't sure what the demand would be, and given that the tri-pod servers only held three dressings, and given that the dressings she was already serving were uniformly popular, Grandma didn't want to abandon one of those in favor of Italian. So, she ordered a case of bottled Italian dressing instead of the big tubs that the other dressings came in. Now when customers came into the café, we presented not only the dressing tri-pod, but also a bottle of restaurant-label Seven Seas Italian dressing, just in case they wanted it.

It didn't sell well. Grandma had worked with her supplier to order less than the minimum, which would have been five cases. They settled on one. Then Grandma had her heart attack and sold the businesses. The restaurant became a florist shop. The equipment was sold, but she was stuck with the Italian dressing, which Mom promptly took home and stored in our basement, along with the Cock-a-Doodle doughnuts that were multiplying in our freezers. We used up a bottle now and then. Mother had intended to take additional bottles to church supper clubs and the like, but there were just not enough events or potlucks to make use of them all. So, what was left of the case was moved to the farm where it sat until the day of the great basement cleanup with its many exciting discoveries. And now we had vintage salad dressing.

A myriad of other things appeared here and there as they continued cleaning out the basement. One of those items was the rose-colored quilt Grandma had had that I loved. After she passed away it had somehow made its way to the farm and was safely stored in a box at the top of one of the stacks in the basement. It was wrapped in tissue with cedar chips interspersed, which would have come from trees in her yard. Grandma had always been very resourceful. There was a $20 bill within the folds along with a yellowing, faded note, "Kelly–Granddaughter Wages."

Lars found an old tractor carburetor. He mentioned it to Dad, who said, "Well, just keep looking. If you look hard enough, you might find the tractor down there, too!"

The biggest surprise was that they found the fireplace, and it still had a log in it! Carbon dating would probably put the petrified object as a relic dating from a Christmas in the early seventies, relatively early in our habitation of the house. Any holiday later than that would have seen us upstairs, because the basement would no longer have been passable not to mention inhabitable. We knew generally where the fireplace was situated—on which wall anyway. But it was wonderful to see the lovely brick exposed once again from its prison. I was disappointed that my jewelry box hadn't turned up, but that also meant that it was probably safely stored upstairs somewhere.

But of course, now, the upstairs was an entirely different matter. The new addition, which was supposed to be the solution to all of Mom's problems, was now home to new solutions of Mom's gathering problem. Stuff was stacked floor to ceiling in there. The floor was passable for maybe the first two weeks after it was completed. But true to obsessive-compulsive disorder, the space became filled again with items that Mom could not find other homes for, or could not bear to get rid of. The unbidden gathering behavior was now on steroids. There was new, uncharted territory to cover. But wouldn't that be the case with the now empty basement? Wouldn't that be a blank canvas now as well?

Dad wanted to go downstairs to check out the basement, but he was afraid to go down the steps. He asked Allison to drive him around from the back of the house to the front so he could see the basement without actually having to walk down the stairs. Of course, they used her car since the one he drove, serving as an annex for mother's hoarding, was full of stuff like it always was, including his winter clothes, which were still taking up residence in the backseat. They were in the plastic bins I'd purchased for him from Walmart five years previously. At least he knew where his clothes were.

Dad had grown noticeably older, his body more frail, but he was still smart. He seemed to be having more obvious episodes of forgetfulness, but generally his mind was still sharp. His hearing was not. During a break from the bonfire, Reese, Allison, and Mom were inside the house trying to have a conversation, but the television was turned up so loud that they could not hear themselves. They asked him to please turn it down. When he didn't respond, Allison went over, took the remote, and turned the volume down. Dad came unglued and grabbed the remote back. *"I am hard of hearing, and if I want the son-of-a-gun turned up loud, I'll turn it up loud!"* he bellowed. Just as suddenly, he switched it off entirely. *"Are you happy now?"* he demanded. But he wasn't finished being angry quite yet.

The general air of untidiness had extended throughout the upstairs and into the refrigerator where some of the food had gone bad. Lars' wife was trying to help by cleaning it out, and Dad had yelled at her for being so "rude." The stress of it all had taken its toll on Dad. On the bright side, much of what had been adding to the clutter were items that Mother had intended to recycle. Yes, actually, she had identified things she could part with. She was a very cooperative participant when Allison told her that she could get some money for the old magazines and so forth because the recycling facility paid by weight. Allison had never seen items leave Mother's hands so quickly.

The insurance adjuster had come on a cloudy Wednesday. We were hopeful that the homeowner's policy would cover the loss. But water that seeps through walls is never covered. I was extremely saddened for them, and for the loss not only of stuff that was just stuff, but also the disappointment and waste of Mom's undying effort of trying to keep it all safe. The fact that Mom had lost control of this, too, just confirmed her life in a word: victim. It would have been nice to see her have total control of one thing, just one thing, once in her life. Dad understood how I felt, but told me to look at the situation with a glass-half-full perspective: "at least we have a clean basement now."

The burning and pitching continued for several days. They never once had to re-light the fire. As if determined to blot out all the bad, old memories, the cathartic flame never died.

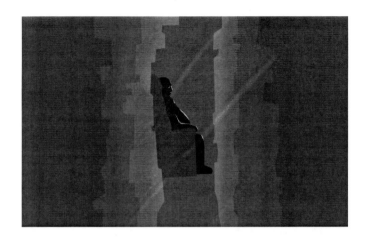

CHAPTER TWENTY
A FRUITLESS EFFORT

Mother took to her bed and slept for two days. It had been cleared of everything except bedcovers. The room remained impassable. The choice was still to walk in and get in bed or to turn around and go back out the door. Dad went to bed as he normally would those two nights and slept as if nothing were unusual. Everybody kept checking on Mother during the day. Her breathing was regular. She was just physically and emotionally spent.

On the third day, she got out of bed, had a cup of tea, and put oil in her ears. She was glad we hadn't moved her spoon out of the cotton balls in the bathroom. She went back to bed and slept again. That afternoon I heard her stirring and went in the bedroom. Dad was out in the living room reading. The TV was off. Otherwise, I'm sure I would not have heard Mother.

I went into the bedroom and saw that she was lying in bed on her back, her arm on her forehead as if trying to shield herself from bright sun. The partly cloudy sky was barely visible through the upper sliver of the window, just discernable above the stack of stuff at the end of the bed. She had a headache.

"Are you okay, Momma?"

"No, sweetheart. Not really."

"Is there anything I can do for you?"

"No, not really."

I sat on the edge of the bed and looked at the woman who had saved me from herself and predators and who had protected me and cared for me in a way that I hadn't understood. I'd thought she was a terrible mother because I didn't remember her attentiveness when I was a baby. I'd felt shoved aside because that's all I could remember. But she had been busy protecting other little ones from dangerous ogres. She had been able to break the cycle of child abuse because she had found another outlet for her anger. The OCD had just been a manifestation. The two horrible creatures that attacked her had stripped her of her self-esteem and dignity, but she more than made up for that in paying forward the kindness of her Sunday schoolteachers. Without them, I'm not sure where life would have taken Mother.

And as I looked down at my mother, I took her hand and told her how sorry I was about everything. I apologized for taking her hassock and throwing it in the old hen house and forgetting to have it reupholstered.

And I told her I was sorry about the basement and that I was sorry about those two men and little Jason and little Stevie and moving to a house she hated. And I stroked her forehead and told her I loved her.

And she looked up at me and told me that she loved me, too.

"It turned out the way it was supposed to," she said. "Life goes on."

"Yes, it does, and tomorrow is a new day," I said. The clouds parted, and a sliver of sunlight over the stacked boxes brightened the room. A bird called from outside, and some leaves rustled in the trees.

"We can probably tackle the upstairs now, Kelly."

I smiled down at her. The lovely silver hair framed her face, which had always been very beautiful. Her eyes were bright and hopeful.

"Yes, Momma, we probably can."

So, when Mom felt better, we made attempts to clean up the upstairs, but it didn't last. The unbidden accumulation of various and assorted treasured objects continued. I came to the disgusting realization that I myself had been part of the problem. I kept running across items that I had sent her, which I hadn't wanted to throw out. And when I had done that, I knew she would keep these things. And keep. And keep. Yet I told myself, perhaps to justify my actions, the things I had sent her I had thought she might use, although they would have had a better use as a donation somewhere else. In spite of myself, knowing that I had been an enabler, I was still disturbed and disappointed that Mother could find so much beauty in so much trash. She would still not seek counseling.

The next time I visited, the new addition to the house was now entirely full of more and more stuff, this time stacked floor-to-ceiling with small paths. The view to the east was now completely obstructed because the windows were blocked. Two of the walls were paneled in the dark paneling that mother loved, and the dark cabinets added to the overall cave-like dwelling. I felt as though I had grown bat wings.

Dad seemed to be doing okay, even though he was back to his small space in the original living room. After all that trouble—the application for the loan, the expense of the new addition, promises from Mother to try to do better, and Dad's excitement that life would now be different for him—it had all gone to dust, and things were exactly the way they had been, except that more space was now full of more clutter. Oh, and now the outside of the house was looking worse because of all of the salvageable stuff that had been moved from the basement, and which was now surrounding the property, making it look more and more like our own personal "redneckville." I was glad that ours was a remote road, and that there weren't too many passers-by.

I hugged Mom and Dad, walked out to the yard and left the place, blessing my sisters for their efforts to keep trying. I had no hope. But no reasonable person would simply hope for change and expect it to occur. What is needed is an executable plan that can be successful, and I knew we didn't have that.

CHAPTER TWENTY-ONE
DAD BECKONS

Another blithering and blubbering phone call from Allison. Dad was near death. Would I come?

I didn't want to go back there. I didn't want to see Dad the way he was now. I selfishly wanted to remember him as sharp, working the Jumbles in the newspaper, and maintaining endless optimism that eventually the house would be clean.

He woke up one morning and knew something was not right. He had spent twenty minutes calling around to find the cheapest ambulance company. Luckily, Allen and Lars happened by and rushed him to the hospital. Dad was admitted with congestive heart failure and pneumonia. When Allison arrived, the hospital staff took her aside and spoke to her in their "nursey" hospital language. Dx and Tx this, and Rx that. Also, did Allison know just what sort of shape Dad's personal hygiene had been in when he was admitted? Well, we think he was probably a mess. Yes, he was. He was wearing the same socks he had worn the last time he was hospitalized, four months earlier. They had not been changed or washed. He had spent the past five days in his chair, un-toileted. Mom couldn't lift him or make him get up, and she had not called for help. We got a wake-up call from the hospital staff: you could be prosecuted for elder neglect, and particularly, you, Reese. She lived closest and was aware of what was going on. What is the state of the house? Allison gave the staff a truthful update. Mother is a hoarder. It's uninhabitable and will have to be cleaned up.

Somehow Dad pulled through. The staff wanted to admit Dad to long-term care instead of letting him go back home. Medicare paid for the first three weeks. Dad did not assimilate. He cried and begged us not to leave him in long-term care to die. He did not want to die in the hospital. He had made up his mind that he was going to get out of there and go home. So, he did not make friends. He would not eat. He would not play checkers or other games.

He was rude to the nurses and kept calling all of them fat asses, or "debi-chon," which he seemed to think meant "fat ass" in Japanese. Dad was spending more and more mental energy back in the Korean War, on R&R in Tokyo. Sometimes he would make inappropriate observations from his hospital bed, which had a full view of the nurse's station when the door was open: "I can tell who each one of those nurses is by the size and shape of their butts. See, that one is Shirley, and that one is Betty. That one over there is Ellen Ann." Or when one of them entered the room and asked Dad to swing his legs back up on the bed, he would hike an elbow under his head and bend one knee up, inquiring, "Do you think I'm sexy?"

Perhaps Dad's weird behavior was borne out of fear that he would have to stay in long-term care because Mom might not do her part to allow him to come home. He was secretly worried that Mother would choose her possessions over him, even though she came over before and after work to see him every day. She was extremely lonely without him. But sometimes when it was just Dad and Allison, he would say things like, "Maybe your mother doesn't want me back home."

Dad would not do anything (besides fret about being tossed out of the house) except to instruct Allison or Reese when such and such credit card bill or propane bill needed to be paid. He had all the due dates completely memorized, and worried that one might be paid late. Just how many credit cards were there? Oh, a few. Dad, do you want us to take over the family finances? Yes.

We discovered a horrifying truth. Dad had eight credit cards. They were all maxed out, and he had been paying the minimum due on each one every month. Mom had one or two as well. She had squirreled away some savings, but it was about one quarter of her total credit card debt. Hers was less than $15,000. Manageable, we thought, but still shocking nonetheless. As to Dad's, I kept receiving text message after text message on my birthday. His total was $63,000. No, now it was $80,000. Oops, more debt was discovered. Add another $16,000 to that. Stop with the texts already! I'm trying to enjoy my birthday. This was more annoying than a lost set of keys and more upsetting than the day Lady got hit by the truck. This wasn't once-and-done. It was a recurring nightmare that would never go away.

They had been paying interest on interest on interest. Neither one had signed up for the governmental drug program available to people aged sixty-five and over: Medicare Part D. Nor did either parent have a medi-gap policy to cover items that Medicare doesn't cover. The debt was mostly for prescription drug expenses. Debt had also been incurred for lots and lots of books and a multitude of angels. I cried until I had no tears left.

The hospital staff was willing to work with us since Dad had wanted to go home instead of staying in long-term care. But drastic measures had to be taken. The house had to be cleaned up once and for all, and it had to stay clean. Dad's doctor was going to make house calls, a further incentive to keep it clean. Dad had to have decent care. His doctor approved hospice for him at home. There would be regular visitors. The family spent the three weeks Dad was hospitalized virtually gutting the upstairs. Stuff was tossed. Allison was ruthless. She mobilized everyone: big people, little people, anybody who was able-bodied helped. But we kept it in the family.

A burn pile was started and used to full advantage. Mother had gone to work, and Allison had told her before she left that the house would look very different when she got back. The army of helpers brought masses of refuse out of the house and pitched it all into the front-end loader that Chip was driving. He made numerous trips out to the burn pile where the mounds and heaps of stuff, or trash—"Hell, it was all trash," according to Allison—was unloaded.

They were careful to keep the items Mother would notice in full view. She asked about the dried eucalyptus that I had given her six years previously, which had still been adorning some old, antique crocks. Well, Mom, we needed to throw out all that old moldy stuff, otherwise Dad would be much sicker. Anything worth saving was carted to the attic, but they were discriminating about that. "If in doubt, throw it out."

Allen and Lars tore out the old kitchen flooring and laid beautiful new vinyl. They painted everything. Lars added more touches here and there. The new addition was spotless. The old part of the upstairs was serviceable and clean, with the exception of the back bedrooms, and the solution for that, until more drastic measures could be taken, was simply to keep the doors shut.

They moved the bed into the main room of the new addition. Dad could do his living there. The new bathroom was now usable as a bathroom again, complete with an old-people's shower, and the laundry room had regained its original purpose as well. A big bin—dark to match the dark décor—was installed just outside the pass-through of the kitchen into the broad hallway of the new addition. They made it easy for her. Mother was encouraged to put recyclables in the recycle bin. The contents would be routinely carted off to Walmart, and she would get some money. Really? I can get money? Yes, Mother, they reminded her, you can get money. This seemed to strike a positive chord once again. But there were also many, many conversations with Mother, reminding her of the threat of Reese being prosecuted and possibly incarcerated if the house slipped back into neglect. *That* was what it finally took.

Dad was as delighted as a child finding a longed-for toy under a Christmas tree when he entered the beautiful house. Allison waved her arm in the direction of the new addition, as if she were about to turn some letters on a TV program, and pointed out how wonderful it now looked. "You have a clean house to live in now, Dad!"

"I have a clean house to die in," he corrected her.

But the reality was that Dad could lie in his bed and watch TV, or if he felt up to it, he could sit in his chair with assistance. It wasn't his same old chair that he had spent the five unattended days in. It was a donation from a friend, but it was in much better condition than his old one. He looked funny sitting in an early American-style chair instead of his La-Z-Boy recliner, but he was clean and comfortable.

When I arrived, I couldn't believe how old my little daddy looked now. He had lost most of his teeth and only had a few stubs in the front of his mouth. They'd spent their money on credit card interest instead of taking care of their personal needs, medications aside. They bought the meds to prolong their lives, which they funded with credit cards, so Mom had to keep working in order to have money to pay the credit card minimums every month. As if ruled by a centrifugal force, they were living a circular life. Lord, what a way to live.

I spent that week, along with my sisters, dealing with bankers and lawyers. In order to pay off the credit card debt, we sold land that had been in the family for over one hundred years. We had no choice. Mom and Dad knew what was going on; we had made sure they were both coherent and lucid when we presented the plan. But it didn't lessen the pain.

Dad had good days and bad. He spent every day I was there lying in bed, watching Fox News. He wasn't well and kept coughing up green phlegm. I told Allison about it. The answer: Dad had chronic bronchitis. Couldn't anything be done? There were two machines near the bed: the familiar oxygen machine, and a new machine, a nebulizer, which he used several times a day for lung treatments. When he wasn't in need of assistance or errand running, I sat quietly and read, trying to block out the loud TV.

He hadn't had a good morning at all. He had decided to turn up the TV and became irate when the remote wasn't working as it should. Reese informed him that he was using the telephone handset instead of the TV remote. She got a good tongue-lashing for that.

One time I glanced over, and he was clearly trying to reach something. I wasn't sure which thing he was trying to retrieve: the oxygen mask or the nebulizer mouthpiece. "What do you need, Dad?" His arm was shaking like he had some kind of palsy. *"Hand me that vibratin' bloody heifer!*" I felt like an idiot. What did that mean? Both machines vibrated to a certain extent. I followed his gaze, and handed him the vibratin' bloody heifer, which as it turned out, was the nebulizer.

After the treatment, when he could speak again, he said, "I'm sorry, Kelly. I didn't mean to yell at you like that." His voice was extremely soft, as if his earlier diatribe had sapped all of his vocal strength.

"It's okay, Dad. I know you don't feel well."

"I'm tired of fighting. My commanding officer kept telling us we had to keep fighting. I don't want to fight anymore," he said in a gravelly voice.

I had had to lean in so that I could hear him. "You have to keep fighting, Dad," I said, probably louder than necessary.

"I don't want to have any more birthdays. I'm tired. I just want to go to sleep. I'm in my nice, clean house now, where I can die in peace."

"You can't leave us now, Dad. You have a job to do."

His voice was barely audible. "I do?" he asked, in a very surprised manner, his dark eyes bright. It was as if I had just informed him that he was about to become a great-grandfather again.

"Yes. Nicole will be very sad if you don't attend her wedding. You must attend." The wedding was a few months away.

"I must attend?"

"Yes, you have to go. You need to be there."

Again the quiet voice, "I do?" But this time, there was hope in it.

"Yes. You have to keep fighting until her wedding. Nicole is expecting to see you there." Nicole was Reese's daughter. We had given Dad a goal. He at least had to try to stay with us for a few more months. Then he wouldn't have to have any more birthdays if he didn't want to.

CHAPTER TWENTY-TWO
SCOUNDRELS AND SCALAWAGS

We arrived early at Mom and Dad's on a fine day in early May. Reese was already at the church seeing to last-minute wedding preparations, and Allison was at the reception hall ensuring that everything was in place. Mom and Dad had asked us to help them get ready and then drive them to the church. My children, Cole, Peter, and Sarah, walked into the house with me.

When I saw Dad, I was as amazed as the day I had first set eyes on the Grand Canyon. He was walking all by himself! No wheelchair, no walker, no lying in bed or being stuck in his borrowed chair hooked up to machines. What's more, not only was he walking, but also he was doing it with a spring in his step and was not carrying his oxygen! Evidently weddings were good for everybody.

Dad was wearing new dress trousers, purchased especially for the occasion, and an old T-shirt. He'd be changing into his good shirt for the wedding once we helped dye his hair. Dad was no longer skipping birthdays or tired of having birthdays. Not only had he decided that birthdays were a good idea, but he also had decided that he wanted to look younger than his eighty years. His hair had just started going gray in the past five years or so. He was one of those lucky souls who'd managed to maintain a youthful appearance for just about forever with no apparent effort.

So, we covered a kitchen chair with a sheet and draped an old towel over Dad's lap in case of some wayward dye. We had opened a small window (not the same window we had shoved the rugs through) for some fresh air. Dad was just a little gray at the temples. It was an easy job and looked great when Sarah and I finished. We handed Dad a mirror. He held the mirror out a little bit to get a wider angle on the view and took a look. He seemed a bit nonplussed, as if he were inspecting a hail-damaged wheat field. Then he leaned back and moved the mirror around, taking it completely away, and then bringing it back into position as if hoping for a different result. He considered himself for a few moments and then delivered the verdict. "Well, now, that doesn't look quite right!" he declared. "In fact, that looks worse than the north end of a south-bound mule!"

I chuckled. "Why do you think that, Dad? It looks wonderful! You look very young."

"Well, yes, and I feel young, too. Just ask Mom. I was chasing her around the house earlier today." Mom blushed and sat very prim in her chair as if that sort of thing had never happened. *Ha-ha, good for him,* I thought.

"Well, Grandpa, I think you look great!" Sarah said.

"I like my hair all right. You girls did a good job on that. But I don't like the way it looks with my beard." He'd grown his beard out, and it was salt-and-pepper, nice and full. It had been neatly trimmed. "What would you think about coloring my beard for me so it matches my hair?"

"Sure, Dad!"

So we began applying the remaining dye to his beard. The process was moving along nicely until Dad decided that the hair dye smell was a little too overpowering on an area so close to his nose. (We didn't get the beard kind of dye; evidently it does exist for that reason.) But he didn't want us to quit. "Can you find something for me to breathe through? A long tube or something?"

Peter said, "Sure, Grandpa! We'll find something for you. Just sit tight!" Cole whispered that somebody had found a beer bong tube during the most recent mass-cleaning purge and knew where it had been stashed in the newly organized house.

When he retrieved it, Dad said, "Ha-ha, you found my old beer bong!" and then looked a little sheepish. "Hey, how'd you know about that?" he asked Cole.

"Let's just say I've been to college," Cole replied.

"So, Grandpa, been to many parties in your lifetime?" Peter asked.

"There isn't a whole lot I haven't done in my lifetime, but don't you be out telling the whole neighborhood. After all, I wasn't born yesterday, you know!" The reality was that everyone probably already knew everything about Dad since the nearest town was the one he had grown up in. They'd know all about his mischief making.

Dad put one end of the tube in his mouth while Peter stood out from him a little bit, directing the free end to the window and the fresh air while we waited for the color to process. Cole ran outside and grabbed the other end, further directing the tube into the fresh prairie air. Sarah thought Dad looked hilarious and took a picture on her cell phone for posterity. Dad was a good sport and thought it was pretty funny himself. Mom laughed, too. Everybody was in a grand mood.

When time was up, we got the mirror again, and Dad took another look. "Well, now, *that's* what I'm talkin' 'bout! *That l*ooks slicker than *snot!*" he said.

"Yeewww, Grandpa!" said Sarah, thoroughly disgusted. We tidied him up, and the boys helped him into his dress shirt. Cole had driven, and we made our way out to the car, with Peter bringing Dad's wheelchair down the dirt path in case he needed it. I took Dad's arm, and Cole and I helped him make his way into the car. Peter got some dirt on his suit as he was putting the wheelchair into Cole's car.

"Oh, I'm sorry, Peter," I said.

Peter brushed his pant leg with his left hand. "It's no big deal, Mom. There's nothing as important as getting Grandpa to the wedding."

And that was the way we all felt. It was a beautiful day, and the wedding was stunning. It was gratifying to see two young people who were truly in love declaring their vows to each other. After the bride and groom made their way down the aisle at the end of the ceremony, it was time to get Dad back down the aisle. He'd decided to use the wheelchair just in case and also had his oxygen tank with him. Mother seemed uncertain what to do and little Mr. Lindquist, Reese's father-in-law, rose to the occasion. "I'll get him!" he squeaked. And the two grandpas came down the aisle together to the delight of the entire congregation.

The next day after all of the festivities had concluded we all made our way out to the farm again around noon. Dad was sitting up in his chair, still looking very dapper with his dark beard and hair. He was eating beef stew and regaling everyone with stories of Al Capone and the Chicago Mafia. Then the conversation turned to other scoundrels and scalawags. Finally, Dad recalled the evening I had come home after tee peeing. Peter, Cole, and Sarah looked absolutely dumbfounded that their little mommy could ever have done such a thing.

I decided it was probably time I told the entire truth and confessed that the evening had involved more than just toilet paper. Everyone listened in rapt attention as I recounted the evening, driving the noisy car and marking Robbie's car with the frozen orange and pineapple juice. I mentioned the special hood ornament as well. Everyone laughed, and Peter said, "Wow, Mom, I never knew you were so cool! You're my new hero!"

"Yeah, Mom, I didn't think you had any friends at all!" Cole added.

"Good for you, Mom!" Sarah said. "Way to kick an old boyfriend back to the curb!" she declared. There seems to be something reassuring at the discovery that your parents were once young and may have done some foolish things.

Dad was laughing heartily as well and began to choke on his roast beef. When we got him settled again, he said, "See, Mother, she takes after me!" with great pride in his voice and laughed some more.

We all gave Dad hugs, kisses, and handshakes. And then we said our good-byes, and Mom walked with us out into the bright sunshine. As we stood on the ridge top, we took in the panoramic horizon, the beautiful greens and soft browns of the land, and the shade of blue that the sky only displays over Kansas. And we filled our lungs with the sweet prairie air, fresh and expectant, once more before we got in the car. And I knew with certainty that if I were to walk back into the house, the air would smell nearly as sweet as the outside breeze, and it would stay that way. Mother had come a long way, and so had Dad. I hoped they both lived to be one hundred years old.

AfTERWORD

According to information appearing on the "Hoarding Overview" page of the I Care Village website *www.icarevillage.com*, in some cases, obsessive-compulsive disorder and other brain-based conditions are often found alongside compulsive hoarding. Although *Collecting Dreams* is not intended to be a scholarly work, I did find researching the condition to be of assistance.

There are many helpful resources within quick and easy reach through the internet. Among these are:

International OCD Foundation *www.ocfoundation.org*. You'll find information regarding what OCD is, resources for assistance, and a hoarding center.

There are a number of useful articles, references, frequently asked questions, and links to other websites regarding hoarding on *www.icarevillage.com*. You'll find everything from causes of hoarding to how to help a family member.

It is true that it took the threat of prosecution in order to change the behavior of the hoarder featured in the book. It is a daily challenge, but having a line of constant visitors has helped. It is true that the hoarder never sought counseling. I would suggest that if you are dealing with a hoarder who is just as strong-willed to at least seek counseling for yourself. According to the internet resources, hoarders often do not recognize that they have a problem. I found it immensely helpful to share my concerns with a professional.

The real-life characters portrayed fictitiously in the book, along with me personally, were encouraged by the hoarding shows on TV. The shows said to me that I was not alone in this struggle; others were out there, and some situations appeared to be far worse than ours. I found this to be perversely reassuring. One of the more interesting episodes featured a psychologist who was the actual hoarder, and who fully knew and understood the roots of hoarding as an addiction to counteract pain (she had been divorced by her husband). As my family and I compared notes about the shows, we noticed that in nearly every episode, the hoarder had suffered some sort of trauma: a divorce, an ill child, etc. This trauma trigger is supported in several sources I researched, is borne out in the story (which I toned down and changed considerably), and happened in real life.

If you have suffered distress or trauma of some sort that has affected the way you live your daily life, know two things:

Whatever you experienced was not your fault; you didn't ask for that, and

Help is available if you want it. Talking to someone else may be beneficial. You are not required to shoulder your burden alone.

All things are possible.

BIBLIOGRAPHY

MedicineNet. William C. Shiel, Jr., MD, FACP, FACR. April 27, 2011. September 16, 2012. *www. medicinenet.com*

Randy O. Frost, Ph.D. Gail Steketee, Ph.D. "About Hoarding."

International OCD Foundation. Elizabeth McIngvale. Jeff Bell. 2012. September 16, 2012. *www. ocfoundation.org*

I Care Village. Sere Halverson. 2010. September 16, 2012. *www.icarevillage.com*

Joni Mitchell, vocal performance of "Both Sides Now," April, 1969, Reprise Records label.